RODNEY HUGHES

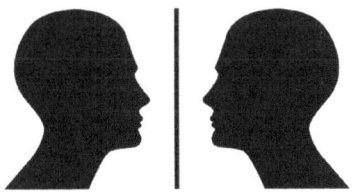

THE UGLY TRUTH ABOUT GETTING HIRED

Author | Executive Recruiter | Interview Strategist

DISCOVER HOW TO LAND THE JOB OF YOUR DREAMS... REGARDLESS OF THE COMPETITION!

Disclaimer

What I'm about to show you is merely a guide. You do not have to follow it verbatim or at all. As a matter of fact, I'm just going to share this information with you as if I were going through the process from beginning-to-end. You can determine if you think it is viable for you or not. If you have any questions or concerns, I would 100% suggest you discuss these ideas with a licensed legal professional prior to implementing. This information is for educational purposes only, and I shall not be held liable for any results that you experience as a result of taking these actions or any other actions in this book as it is ONLY meant for educational purposes only.

THE UGLY TRUTH ABOUT GETTING HIRED
Author Rodney Hughes

Cover illustration by: Rodney Hughes
First printed: January 2018
Atlanta, Georgia

The Ugly Truth About Getting Hired book is available at special discounted rates when purchased in bulk for premiums, sale promotions, fund-raising and/or educational use. Special editions or book excerpts can also be created to specifications.

All rights reserved. No part of this book may be used or reproduced in any form or by any means, electronic or mechanical, including photo-copying, recording or by any information storage and retrieval system without prior written permission of the Author except for the inclusion of brief quotations in a review.

ISBN: 978-0-692-99171-8
Printed in the United States of America
Design & Text Design by Rodney Hughes

Disclaimer: The information contained in this book are based on research and personal experience of the Author and offer no guarantee of outcomes/results. Please give careful consideration to your particular life circumstances. The concepts shared in this book are not intended as a substitute for hard work, determination, dedication, and discipline that is required to achieve results in the employment process. Readers should take from this material only those parts that are appropriate for them and assume personal responsibility for whatever guidelines they select. Should a reader have concerns regarding the concepts shared within this book, the Author and Publisher strongly suggest that you consult with another competent and trusted legal professional. The Author and Publisher shall have neither liability, nor responsibility, to any person with respect to any loss or damage caused or alleged to be caused directly or indirectly by the information in this book. This book is strictly for educational purposes only.

DEDICATION

I dedicate this book to Rodney Hughes III *(3.0)*. Son… One day you'll have to maneuver the treacherous employment landscape *(either as an Employer or as an Employee)*, and when you do, hopefully this book will help you effectively acquire the success that you're looking for. This book is like a treasure map… It is designed to help you find whatever treasures you're looking for in the employment process. My hope is that the concepts that I share with you in this book will give you a competitive advantage as you grow into the powerful man that God has blessed you to become.

Success is not easy, but if you're willing to pay the price, you can have anything that you focus on attaining in this world. Always remember Son, the only things that pay in life are the things you get done! Learn these concepts, apply these concepts, and do what is necessary *(within the rules and laws of the land)* to get the job done. I always have, and I always will love you son!

FREE INTERVIEW PREP VIRTUAL TRAINING

•••

Discover extremely effective strategies that will help you seamlessly maneuver the job interview process like a pro!

Dear Success-Minded Friend:

Because you purchased this book, I'm going to give you (FREE) lifetime access to a virtual training platform called INTERVIEW PREP UNIVERSITY. This virtual training platform is specifically designed to walk you step-by-step through the job interview process and help you avoid the major pitfalls that cause most candidates to fail miserably in the job interview process…

Here's a quick glance at what you'll learn in Interview Prep University…

- **COURSE 1:** Interview Scheduling Course
    - Learn how to quickly schedule interviews with top companies.
- **COURSE 2:** Telephone Interview Course
    - Learn how to avoid the common telephone interview mistakes.
- **COURSE 3:** Onsite Interview Course
    - Learn how to effectively sell yourself during a job interview.
- **COURSE 4:** Compensation Course
    - Learn how to negotiate top-dollar when getting an offer.

How to use this virtual course effectively?

The best way to get maximum value from this virtual course is to start by completely reading this book. This book will serve as the foundation for what you're going to learn in this virtual course. Once you've read the book, you can use this platform in various ways. You can go through the whole course in one evening, pace yourself and do a section a day, or jump straight to a certain section of this course that you think is most applicable to your concerns. Remember… This virtual course is designed to supplement the ideas, concepts, and strategies that are shared in this book.

How do you gain instant access to Interview Prep University?

Go to ➔ www.InterviewPrepUniversity.com

TABLE OF CONTENTS

How to effectively use this book for employment success. (Pg. 9)

Introduction: The top 3 reasons you should read this book! (Pg. 12)

PART 1: MASTERING THE INNER GAME OF EMPLOYMENT SUCCESS

CH 1	The most important guiding principle to employment success	(Pg. 22)
CH 2	The single most valuable attribute of an ideal Candidate	(Pg. 27)
CH 3	This is a game of perception… not fact	(Pg. 32)
CH 4	Always remember… We live in a world of good enough	(Pg. 36)
CH 5	See the world as it really is… Not the way you want it to be	(Pg. 41)
CH 6	Destroying competition… Lead with value & exceed with value	(Pg. 46)
CH 7	You must be prepared to kiss a lot of frogs	(Pg. 52)
CH 8	You must learn how to be the purple zebra	(Pg. 57)
CH 9	Be disciplined in this world or be disciplined by this world	(Pg. 62)
CH 10	Lions & Gazelles… Embrace the path of massive action	(Pg. 67)

PART 2: MASTERING THE OUTER GAME OF EMPLOYMENT SUCCESS

CH 11	It's not rocket science, but it is a science	(Pg. 74)
CH 12	PHASE I: Performing Strategic Recon	(Pg. 78)
CH 13	PHASE II: Becoming The Ideal Blip	(Pg. 94)
CH 14	PHASE III: The Secrets Of Interviewing Mastery	(Pg. 103)
CH 15	PHASE IV: Creating A Sense Of Certainty	(Pg. 125)
CH 16	PHASE V: The Magic Is In The Follow-Up	(Pg. 132)
CH 17	PHASE VI: How To Get What You Really Want	(Pg. 138)
	Conclusion: Take the EASY STREET to massive success	(Pg. 144)

> "I FEAR NOT THE MAN WHO HAS PRACTICED 10,000 KICKS ONCE, BUT I FEAR THE MAN WHO HAS PRACTICED ONE KICK 10,000 TIMES"
>
> ~ Bruce Lee

How To Use This Book Most Effectively?

If you're reading this book right now, it tells me a lot about you! It tells me that you're serious about improving your life, that you have a burning desire to create a better employment situation for you and your family, and that you have the capability and potential to learn and grow. So, if you're going to take the time to read this book, I want to make sure that you use it as effectively as you possibly can.

The very first thing that I want you to understand is that this book is merely a tool. A tool that you can use to acquire and develop extremely effective and practical strategies for maneuvering through the employment process. Now that you understand that this book is a tool, you need to also understand that tools are only as valuable as its wielder. Let me explain…

Let's use a hammer as an example. A hammer is a popular tool that people use to apply force and give a heavy blow to an object. For us, the hammer is a tool that both professionals and amateurs can use to fulfill their purpose. Professionals and amateurs have the right to buy this tool and use it however they see fit; but have you ever wondered why or how two different people can use the exact same tool(s), yet one person is able to extract way more value out of that tool than the next?

Think about it for a second. An amateur can go to the store, purchase a hammer, go home, and use that hammer to potentially save a couple hundred dollars on general home improvements. At that very same moment, a professional can go to the same store at the same time, and purchase the same hammer, yet get drastically different results. While the amateur is using this tool to save a couple hundred dollars, that professional can and will likely use that same hammer to generate thousands (*if not millions*) more in value. See, the professional has probably invested a lot of time and effort into repeatedly using this tool so that he/she could effectively use it in the marketplace to extract higher levels of value. What's the moral of this story? It's not the tool, but it's the wielder that creates value!

If you want to extract high levels of value from this book, you must read this book many times. Like the old saying goes, "REPETITION is the mother of all skill". By repetitively reading this book, you'll be able to gain a deeper level of understanding of the ideas, concepts, and strategies that are being shared. Repetitively reading this book will hopefully be like repetitively watching your favorite movie. Each time you read this book, you'll notice something different that you didn't quite notice before. This deeper level of understanding will make it easier for you to execute on the information in the future. And we all know that action (execution) is the only thing that leads to positive results.

Tools are designed to make it easier for you to get a desired result. If you use a tool every once in a while, then you'll probably notice that your results are only a little bit better. If you use a tool over and over again, then you'll probably notice that you're able to get much greater results than most of the people you know. Determine how you're going to use this tool! Are you going to use this book to get slightly better results, or are you going to really apply yourself and learn how to use this book to dramatically improve your employment situation? It's your choice!

"THE DEGREE TO WHICH A PERSON CAN GROW IS DIRECTLY PROPORTIONAL TO THE AMOUNT OF TRUTH HE CAN ACCEPT ABOUT HIMSELF WITHOUT RUNNING AWAY"

~ Leland Val Van De Wall

INTRODUCTION: The top 3 reasons why you should read this book & continue reading this book until its concepts become emblazoned in your mind

•••••

REASON #1: The 99.9% Rule…

Your success in the job interview process is 100% your responsibility. When it comes to the job interview process, there is no knight in shining armor. There are no cheat codes that you can take advantage of to eliminate competition and obstacles in your path. There are no super heroes with special powers that are going to come out of nowhere and help you land the job of your dreams. Like the old saying goes, "If it is to be… It's up to me!" You have to step up and pay the price to create the employment success that you desire because no one else is going to do it for you.

Many years ago, I came up with a concept that has always helped me keep things in perspective as it relates to my job interview success. I called this concept the 99.9% rule. This is arguably one of the most important rules that I've focused on while striving to improve my own job interview skills. I'd even go to the extent of saying that this has been a very important rule for my life in general. The rule is very simple-- **easily 99.9% of all the people on planet Earth could care less if I ever accomplish my employment goals, and furthermore, could probably care**

less if I ever lived to see another day and died under the worst possible circumstances. I know what you're probably thinking at this point. Whoa! That's a little over the top Rodney! If that's what you're currently thinking, I completely understand; but let me explain the significance of this rule.

Let's start with the purpose of this rule. The purpose is to help you focus on the importance of ruthless personal responsibility. When going through the job interview process, it's so easy to want to blame other people and other situations for your lack of results. Think about it: We blame other people for stopping us from getting the promotion that we desired. We blame our boss for not seeing the value that we bring to the table. We blame the people that we interview with at a new company for not asking good questions through the interview, so they can see our true value. We blame the testing that a company may require us to do for being bias and insignificant. We will literally come up with every possible excuse in the world to help us feel better about not accomplishing our employment goals, but there's one major issue with this list. Like the late, great Jim Rohn once said, "You're not on that list!"

You'll never start accomplishing your employment goals until you get to a place where you start exercising ruthless personal responsibility. The 99.9% rule is designed to help you wrap your head around the importance of ruthless personal responsibility. Picture this: it is currently estimated to be over seven billion people on planet earth. Nowadays, we hear people say the word billion a lot, but I want you to take a moment to *really* think about how big a billion is! For easy math, let's just say that there are seven billion people on planet earth. Now let's figure out what 0.01% of seven billion is. That's 700,000!

Do you know and have a personal relationship with 700,000 people? It can likely be argued that nobody that has ever graced planet Earth that has had a personal relationship with 100,000 people, let alone 700,000 people-- and we're only talking about 0.01% of the world's population! Do you even know 0.0001% of the people on planet earth personally *(by the way… that's approximately 7,000 people)*? Unless you're some type of super celebrity or something, it's pretty likely that you don't personally know 7,000 people. So, what's my point you ask? The overwhelming majority of people on planet Earth don't even know you exist, and definitely don't care about your dreams and ambitions as it relates to your employment success. As a matter of fact, they could probably care less if you lived to see another day and died under the worst possible circumstance. If you died tomorrow *(assuming that somehow they learned about your death)*, most of the people would likely just think to themselves something like, "That's so unfortunate… *(3 seconds later…)* Baby, what are we eating for dinner later on this evening?"

I know what I'm saying here may come across a little ugly, but this is the ugly truth about the job interview process and life. Most people don't really care about you; they only care about themselves and the people closest to them. That's it! When it comes to your employment dreams, goals, and desires, you have to realize and drill it into your head that most of the people simply don't care! If you're going to make your employment dreams come true, then it's going to be 100% up to you. That's what ruthless personal responsibility is all about.

From this day forward, you have to commit to taking full responsibility for all aspects of your employment results and any other results that you want in your personal life. Never allow yourself to blame anyone or anything *(outside of yourself)* for the results-- or lack thereof-- that you have generated in both your career and your personal life. If you can't get yourself to a space of ruthless personal responsibility, then there is literally nothing that I or anyone else can do to help you improve your employment results because you're going to self-sabotage your efforts either consciously or subconsciously. BUT... If you're *willing* to commit to ruthless personal responsibility, then this book might end up being the most valuable book that you've ever read. The contents of this book will help you take control of your employment destiny and exponentially increase the odds of finding and obtaining the job of your dreams!

REASON #2: The competition is fierce, and only getting fiercer...

I want you to take some time to really think about the current employment situation. In my opinion, 2007 was the year that officially changed the employment landscape in the United States *(and the world for that matter)* forever! In 2007, we started to go into one of the worst economic contractions that we've ever seen since the Great Depression. However, I feel it was much worst! Back during the Great Depression, there wasn't nearly as much access to information and technology as there is today. If someone wanted to puke information (fear) on the American people, they had to make a considerable investment in time and money to do so. Nowadays, anybody with a cell phone can potentially puke information (fear) on the American people. In fact, they can practically do this very little effort, and in most cases, for free.

Not only is there a great deal of access to information nowadays, but there's also a great deal of technological advancements that we have created to help solve many problems that weren't viable during the Great

Depression. Back in 2007 when the recession started to hit, many organizations in America were able to have access to technological advancements that could replace the work of many of their employees. When the Great Depression hit, companies didn't have nearly as many resources that they could rely upon to make it through those tough times and become profitable again. During that economic downturn, there were major incentives to figure out ways to make it through those tough times and then start hiring a great deal of employees back for the sake of profitability. That's just not the case anymore.

Since the recession in 2007, companies have been forced to learn how to operate leaner. So now you'll find that many companies that were forced to reduce their headcounts have started to make significant investments in figuring out how they can leverage technological resources that are currently available to them in order to operate a highly profitable business without having to have such a large workforce. Essentially, they're making it so that they won't have to be responsible for the large overhead that comes with those employees. Employees are typically the most expensive investment that any company will have to make, so if companies can leverage technological resources that don't require nearly as much investment, then you better believe that that is what companies are going to do.

Now after that whole spill, let's bring it back home. How does this impact competition in the job marketplace? Believe it or not, it actually impacts the job market in a very dramatic way. There was already a lot of competition in the job market before the recession ever hit, but now the competition is fierce. Unfortunately, it's only going to get fiercer because of technology! Why? After the recession began and many companies started going out of business or reducing their headcounts by the thousands, it impacted the supply and demand equation in the job market. In a very short period of time, an already saturated job market became even more saturated with people that had great backgrounds and were willing to accept more responsibilities for less pay. At that time, people who had amazing backgrounds were starting to apply for the same jobs that people coming fresh out of college were competing for to make ends meet. As you can well imagine, many companies started to take advantage of that situation.

Even to this day, you can find people who are willing to settle for less for the sake of survival. Things have never officially rebounded from an employment perspective because there is no need for companies to go back to very large workforces when they can simply invest in one technological item that can do the jobs of many. While I hate to be all doom and gloom, the reality is that things are only going to get worse! Technology is starting to really focus hard on making advancements in the Artificial Intelligence (A.I.) space. That's going to be a whole different ballgame! Right now, your job is fairly protected if it couldn't be fully duplicated by a machine. When they get to the point of having machines that can actually think (and it's looks like many tech companies are starting to go in that direction), even more jobs will be lost, and the job market will become even more saturated with talent! Just look at what they're trying to do from a technological perspective to the trucking industry as we speak. You need to get on the ball!

I'm not sharing this with you to make you scared. I'm sharing this with you to help you understand how important it is that you start focusing on developing your employment skills now! There's nothing that you can do to change the tide of technology in the employment space. All you can do is try to acquire the skill sets that will allow you to have an unfair advantage in the job market both now and in the future. Like I keep stressing to you, competition is tough now, and it's going to get much tougher. The people that will be freaking out as competition gets tougher will be the people who never made the investments to make sure that their employment skills are well above average. People with average or poor employment skills are going to get absolutely crushed as technology continues to advance. Reading this book and rigorously executing the concepts, techniques, and strategies presented within its pages will help you confidently maneuver the treacherous employment environment as competition continues to elevate.

REASON #3: You've got to be tough if you're going to be stupid…

One of the best quotes that I've ever heard came from someone I consider to be a mentor of mine, and his name is Gary Halbert. I've never actually met Gary, but I remember watching a video of his on YouTube where he uttered the expression, "You've got to be tough if you're going to be stupid". I personally thought that was a very profound statement. He was using this expression in the context of teaching people how to learn marketing strategies that could help his class participants to drive more sales to their business. In essence, he was trying to articulate to these participants that you can learn how to win in business the hard way by making mistake after mistake and wasting countless minutes, hours, or even years trying to figure out how to be successful OR… You can learn from him and his mistakes, and avoid making the same mistakes to generate success in less time.

If you've even made it this far in this book, then that tells me that you're eager to learn something from this book that can help you or someone you know get greater results in the job interview process. By reading this book, you'll no longer be ignorant to the concepts, techniques, and strategies that some of the most skillful interviewees are using to gain an unfair advantage in the job marketplace. But once you have this information, choosing not to apply it rigorously in job interview scenarios to increase your odds of landing the position is just plain stupid! The dictionary defines stupid as "Having or showing a great lack of intelligence or common sense". Once you learn and internalize the information in this book, it will be like having your own personal cheat sheet in the job interview process. You'll be able to hunt down the opportunities that are right for you and control outcomes in many cases.

Gary's sentiment is equally as applicable to the contents of this book as it was to his marketing information. By reading the contents of this book, you'll know more about creating opportunities and positioning yourself as the ideal candidate than most people will ever know. To take the time out to learn this valuable information, and then not apply this information rigorously is just plain stupid. This book is almost as powerful as insider trading *(without breaking the law of course)*, so there really is no excuse for stupidity. Knowing this… If you *still* choose to embrace the path of stupidity, just know, "You got to be tough if you're going to be stupid"! Make the decision now to internalize the concepts in this book and look for every way possible to apply this information. This book will help you far beyond your wildest imagination!

PART 1: Mastering The Inner Game Of Employment Success

"THE ONLY THINGS THAT PAY IN LIFE ARE THE THINGS YOU GET DONE"

~ Rodney Hughes

CHAPTER 1:

The MOST IMPORTANT GUIDING PRINCIPLE to employment success

•••••

This will be the cornerstone of any success that you'll be able to create for yourself in the job interview process...

What I'm about to share with you in this chapter is by far the single most important principle that you can ever grasp in the job interview process: Hence why I put it first. While I'm going to share with you concepts, techniques, and strategies that can help you exponentially improve you job interview results in way less time, you've got to wrap your head around this one principle to get the full benefit of any of the other information that is shared in this book. Yes, this principle is just that important!

The title of this principle is simply, "Solving Problems". The single most important guiding principle that you should focus on in the job interview process to exponentially improve your results is solving problems. Do you realize that there is only ONE reason on God's green earth why any employer would ever hire an employee? The answer: he/she has a series of problems that need to be solved. THAT'S IT!

This one principle is so important that if you don't understand it, you will surely struggle in the job interview process and mess up many opportunities. The huge mistake that most candidates make when they're going through the job interview process is that they focus solely on trying to solve their own problems. They want to make sure that their compensation is sufficient. They want to make sure that they would have great healthcare. They want to make sure that they have adequate vacation. They want to make sure that they like the people that they'll be working with. They want to make sure that they like the facility. You get my drift.

Please listen to me, and listen to me clearly. The people that are involved in the hiring process, especially the hiring decision maker(s), COULD CARE LESS about helping you solve your problems UNTIL they feel confident and convinced that you can help them solve theirs FIRST! I promise you that the hiring decision maker(s) didn't get up this morning thinking to themselves, "I can't wait to find someone I can give a great compensation package to and other amazing perks just for joining my team". There's probably at least a 99.99999% chance that these people woke up trying to figure out how they can solve their problems, not yours!

If you can wrap your head around the guiding principle that the ONLY reason anyone would ever HIRE YOU is because they want to solve THEIR problems, NOT YOURS… You can start to purposefully take decisive actions that will help an employer realize that you're focused on doing just that. By doing so, you'll start to notice that your effectiveness in the job interview process will start to skyrocket! You will stand out from most of your competition because most of your competition will still be stuck on me, me, and me. While your competition is primarily focused on self-advancement, you'll be focused on figuring out creative ways to help your company of interest realize that you can help them solve their problems. This simple change in focus will naturally cause employers to become attracted to you as the ideal candidate.

This principle is so powerful that it can even work outside of the traditional job interview process. I was recently having a conversation with one of my best friends where we were discussing the effectiveness of this principle in different settings. He asked me how this principle could potentially be applied to the job fair environment where there are a lot of distractions and many people that are trying to get the same jobs that you're interested in. I gave him a scenario of how I would apply this principle to stand out.

I would go up to a recruiter at a job fair and instead of asking them if they're hiring or asking about other insignificant things that really don't matter, I would introduce myself, let the recruiter know my area of specialty, and ask if they currently have a need in my area. Up to this particular point in time, I haven't really used this guiding principle, but based on the response of the recruiter; I will have an opportunity to stand out tremendously. If the recruiter says that his organization might have a need for my area of specialty, then I would ask, "If I could help the hiring manager for this position solve one or two major challenges over the next twelve months that would make the decision to hire me one of the best decisions that he or she has ever made, what would those be?"

Let me explain the significance of asking a question like this in this scenario. This is the type of question that will help this recruiter easily understand that you're the type of person that would be focused on helping them solve their problems! This question also forces the recruiter to not only see you as someone they have already decided to hire, but also someone who has solved important problems so well that he/she might consider you the best hiring decision they've ever made. Asking this type of question will also help you stand out like an eight-foot tall person in a room full of little people. There is a very low likelihood that this recruiter has ever been asked a question like this at a job fair. That makes you memorable! Regardless of the answer that is provided, there is a very good chance that they'll remember you out of the sea of hundreds of people that they'll likely meet at this type of an event. Why? Because you would have probably been the only person that demonstrated a focus on helping the company solve its problem!

Hopefully this example will help you start to wrap your head around the extremely valuable nature of this guiding principle. As we continue forward in this book, I want you to keep this principle at the forefront of your mind. You'll start to notice, especially when we start digging into the specifics, that this guiding principle is woven into the fabric of each and every concept, technique, and strategy that I share with you. This guiding principle is at the core of the entire job interview process because an employment opportunity can't exist without there being a problem that needs to be solved. By knowing this, you can start to quickly position yourself from the very beginning of the job interview process as the ideal candidate because you can not only demonstrate to them that you're interested in helping them solve their problems, but you're also competent enough to help solve them.

"WITH THE RIGHT ATTITUDE, HUMAN BEINGS CAN MOVE MOUNTAINS. WITH THE WRONG ATTITUDE, THEY CAN BE CRUSHED BY THE SMALLEST GRAIN OF SAND"

~ Jim Rohn

CHAPTER 2:

The single most important attribute of an IDEAL CANDIDATE

•••••

It's easy to find Candidates with great skills … what's hard to find is a Candidate with a great attitude.

We've all probably heard the expression before, "your attitude will determine your altitude". While I'm sure that sounds very cliché, I assure you that's a very true statement when it comes to the job interview process. Your attitude will either make or break you in the job interview process. If you have a positive attitude, you may be able to connect on a much deeper level with the hiring decision makers. If you have a negative attitude, then it will not typically matter how skillful you are at the execution of your craft, and the hiring decision makers will likely pass on you.

Why is having a great attitude so vital to the job interview process? Before I immediately jump into some of the more obvious areas of importance, I want to give you some context first. As mentioned previously, the only reason why any employer would ever hire and pay someone is because they desire to solve a problem. When solving a problem in your business, HOW you solve a problem is just as important as the problem itself. No Hiring Manager in the world wants to hire someone to solve one particular problem, and then end up having three or four additional problems as a result.

As an example, let's imagine that you owned a small consulting firm with approximately 15 dedicated employees. You've consistently grown your business over the last 10 years since you first started, and now you're interested in hiring a new Sales Director because you want someone to be fully dedicated to leading your team to explosive sales results. You and your leadership team had a strategic plan and decided that you wanted to grow the business from a $3 million company to an $8 million company over the next 3 years. As a result of your strategic initiative *(aka problem)*, you and your team decided that your firm needs a Sales Director who has been there and done that. You're looking for someone who knows how to drive results in a short period of time.

Now, let's imagine that you've started promoting this role on all the major job boards and have been able to narrow 500 resume submissions down to two legitimate candidates. Both of these candidates have very impressive skills with over 15 years of experience working with consulting organizations similar to yours and have the ability to successfully lead their sales forces to exponentially increasing their sales performances. Now, say that the ONLY real difference between these two candidates was their attitude. After asking a series of behavioral interview questions *(which I'll explain in much greater detail later in this book)*, you determined that one candidate came across more like a dictator that believed in ruling with an iron fist and would do anything necessary to accomplish the goal, while the second candidate seemed to be much more of a compassionate leader that would collaborate with the team and then get down n' dirty while leading from the front. As a hiring decision maker in this particular scenario, which candidate would you likely go with?

If you had a close-knit group that you wanted to remain intact after accomplishing such an ambitious target, then which candidate would likely be more appealing to you? I typically don't like to assume, but since I can't get an immediate response because you're actively reading this book, I'm going to use my deductive reasoning skills and guess that you would have likely chosen the second candidate. Why? Presumably, because both candidates seem to have competency around accomplishing a task of this nature, then your primary determining factor will likely be around culture (or how many people like to call it… "fit"). In this situation, I wouldn't think that you would want to accomplish your target while leaving a trail of blood behind you. You've worked hard over the years to grow a successful consulting firm, and I'm sure that you'll want to keep that team intact.

Since I've been helping people improve their employment skills over the years, I can't even begin to tell you how many candidates that I've seen get rejected for not being a "good fit" for that particular organization. Fit can oftentimes be very difficult to identify as a candidate prior to entering into the job interview process where you start actively engaging with hiring decision makers. In the example above, we were talking about a small company that had a tight knit group. A hiring decision maker in that scenario would likely not want someone to come in and take a "by any means necessary" approach towards getting results. While accomplishing the goal is definitely important, this hiring decision maker would likely want to do so without a lot of collateral damage. This is why the second candidate would have likely been extended the offer as opposed to the first. As a candidate, you must understand that each company is going to have a certain type of culture that they want to establish or maintain. That means that each hiring decision maker will likely have a different type of "fit" that they're looking for from an ideal candidate.

While I would never tell you or expect you to lie, exaggerate, or bend the truth for the purpose of getting a job, it is very important that you understand that "fit" expectations are subjective from company-to-company. You must be prepared to analyze what each hiring decision maker is looking for from a "candidate fit" perspective by asking strategic questions and being able to use your active listening skills to deduct a reasonable conclusion. Later in this book, I'll go over some very specific strategies you can use to gain a better understanding of what type of fit a hiring decision maker might be looking for so you can better align yourself in the interviewing process; but for now, I just want you to understand how significant having a great attitude is. Understand that hiring decision makers are going to be analyzing your attitude from the moment you walk through the door until the end of the interview process to determine if you would be a great "fit" for their team.

"EVERYTHING WE HEAR IS AN OPINION, NOT A FACT. EVERYTHING WE SEE IS A PERSPECTIVE, NOT THE TRUTH"

~ Marcus Aurelius

CHAPTER 3:

This is a GAME OF PERCEPTION... Not fact

●●●●●

The best interviewees in the world are phenomenal when it comes to controlling their perception in the job interview process...

The employment process is like playing the ultimate game of perception. In this process, if you're off by even a little bit from a perception perspective, you'll likely be eliminated from the job consideration process swiftly. I've often told people that this is one of the most unforgiving processes you'll ever go through. I've seen candidates with phenomenal backgrounds quickly taken out of the consideration process for frivolous reasons. If you want to dramatically improve your odds while maneuvering through the job interview process, then you're going to have to put an immense amount of energy and focus towards controlling the perception that you create in the minds of the hiring decision makers.

Have you ever heard the expression; "God is in the details"? This is an old saying that people use from time to time to emphasize the idea that details matter, and that whatever you're doing should be done thoroughly and with the utmost attention. When it comes to controlling your perception in the job interview process, you need to understand that every single detail matters! To overlook even one detail in this entire process could come back to haunt you. I know this might sound a little over-dramatic, but I assure you that what I'm saying is very true. From the moment that you become a blip on the radar of a potential employer, every detail has great value in the process.

Perception is important to the job interview process because the main constraint is time. Employers are forced to take extremely limited information and make a judgment as to whether or not someone is really worth their investment. Even if a candidate claims to have amazing skills on their resume, that candidate could very well be making everything up to get a job. Think of it this way: when an employer decides that they want to hire someone to help them solve their problem(s), they're putting a large amount of finances at considerable risk based on having a very limited amount of information about that candidate. Even if an employer is paying minimum wage, an employer is putting a considerable amount of capital at risk with absolutely no guarantee that they'll ever be able to recoup their investment. As a result, this type of risk can tend to make some hiring decision makers hypersensitive about drawing negative conclusions about the perception that a candidate creates in the job interview process.

Let me be clear about something before we move any deeper into this subject… Again, I never want you to lie, embellish, or stretch the truth about your background in order to create the ideal perception. Lying in order to create an ideal perception is not right, and will likely come back to bite you in your bum. As it relates to creating the right perception, I want you to focus on drawing out and positioning your background and everything you do in the most positive light possible. Your goal for creating great perception in the job interview process should be to make it easy for people to quickly see your value.

Again, lying is bad. Don't do it. Instead, I want you to focus on the details so you can create the most conducive environment for building a great perception in the mind of any hiring decision maker that you interact with. I have a great analogy that I would like to share with you that does a great job of articulating my point. Effectively maneuvering through the job interview process is very similar to effectively maneuvering through the early phases of starting a romantic relationship. When you first start dating someone, you will typically have very little information to go off of on the person you're dating. You can't really control whether that person will ultimately end up liking you, but you can focus on the details to increase the odds of that person liking you.

You can make sure that your hair is done nicely, you wear your best outfit, you put on a nice smelling fragrance, you bring mints, your car is clean, your house is spotless, etc. These are all very practical things that you can do to control the perception that you're creating in the mind of the person you're trying to successfully date. None of these things will require you to lie, exaggerate, or stretch the truth, but all of these things will help you to increase your odds of success. Similarly, when you're maneuvering through the employment process, there are many things that you can do to control the perception that you create in the minds of the hiring decision makers. It is 100% your responsibility to do your best to control the perception you create with the limited information that you present so you can increase your odds of getting hired. Later in this book, I'll be breaking down specific tactics and strategies that you can implement to create a very positive perception for yourself.

"PERFECTION IS MAN'S ULTIMATE ILLUSION. IT SIMPLY DOESN'T EXIST IN THE UNIVERSE... IF YOU ARE A PERFECTIONIST YOU ARE GUARANTEED TO BE A LOSER IN WHATEVER YOU DO"

~ David D. Burns

CHAPTER 4:

Always remember… We live in a world of good enough

•••••

Don't allow the myth of perfection to discourage you from executing the powerful strategies in this book. The truth of the matter is that you only need to be good enough to get amazing results!

If you're anything like me, sometimes you start receiving a lot of information and get to feeling overwhelmed. After all, you have a boatload lot of new, valuable information, and you're trying to make sense of it all. Trust me, I've been there!

It's okay if you feel a little overwhelmed at first because some of the concepts, techniques, and strategies that I'm sharing with you will require you to get outside of your comfort zone. In my opinion, it can be very difficult for some people to get outside of their comfort zone because they have a mindset of perfectionism. They tend to never feel like they're ready to take action until they feel like there is a great chance that they'll do something perfectly. They never take the time needed to sit back and accept the realistic perspective that perfection has never existed in the past, and it will never exist in the future.

Perfection is a false narrative that will keep you trapped where you are in life. When I think about perfection, it makes me think about something I heard a very successful Network Marketer, Don Bradley, once mention in a training event... Don said, "You have to avoid having a P.O.O.R mentality in life. P.O.O.R is an acronym that stands for Passing Over Opportunities Repeatedly". This statement is vitally important when I think about the role that perfection has played in my life from time to time and how it has limited the lives of many other people. Arguably, perfection is one of the leading causes of people passing over opportunities repeatedly.

When I look over my life, the only real regret that I have is that there have been times that I have made the conscious choice to compromise on things I really wanted because I was committed to the idea of perfection. This perfection mindset led me to feel as though I was never ready. Perfection has caused me to second guess my decision and hesitate when I should have gone full steam ahead. The idea of perfection has caused me to miss out on opportunities that I can never get back. To be blunt: perfection is a robber of dreams and amazing experiences!

When it comes to getting hired, you can't afford to have a mindset of perfection. Having a mindset of perfection in the employment process will cause you to never take action, and hence, never have the opportunity to get hired. You have to understand that perfection doesn't exist, and you have nothing to lose and everything to gain. After years of helping people from all types of backgrounds successfully maneuver the job interview process, I can assure you that I've never seen anyone-- including myself-- maneuver through the job interview process perfectly. Achieving perfection in the job interview process should not be your focus. Figuring out everything you can do to increase your odds should be the main thing you focus on. Every person I know that is really good at maneuvering through the job interview process can think 3-4 steps ahead about ways to increase their odds without ever striving for perfection. These people were just doing their best to be "good enough" to get the job!

I originally got this concept of being good enough from my dad when I was a teenager. I had a crush on a girl I went to school with, and I really wanted to ask her out on a date. My dad asked me why I didn't just approach her and strike up a conversation with her and see where it goes. I told my dad that I literally don't have any idea about what to say. He could see that I was driving myself slightly crazy trying to think about the perfect way that I could go about asking this girl out without making myself look dumb. He brought up an observation that would change the way I thought about perfection forever.

My dad told me that it seemed like I was looking for perfection in a perfection-less world. He said that the only way I can break out of this perfectionist mindset was to start looking for the imperfections. By observing imperfections, you can lessen the pressure of feeling like you have to be perfect. He went on to explain that he never felt like he was the most attractive man in the world, but that never mattered to him because he just wanted to look good enough to have a shot with the type of women that he was attracted to. He also gave me another example. He said, "Do you think a billionaire cares whether another billionaire found a smarter way to get to a billion dollars? Do you think Oprah cares that Warren Buffet or Bill Gates may have found a smarter way to get to a billion dollars? Of course not!"

Just as a point of clarification: my dad wasn't implying that I should always look for imperfection in other people. He was implying that if you feel the pressure of perfection, then you should step back and observe the imperfection in the situation as a whole whether it's other people or other things. This way of thinking is especially valuable in the job interview process. If you're stuck on perfection, then you may never take the necessary risks to get the results that you desire. The genius about embracing a "world of good enough" mentality is that it will literally free you up to take the kinds of actions that will positively separate you from all of your other competition in the job interview process.

"YOU CAN ONLY DEPEND ON YOURSELF. THE CALVARY AIN'T COMING"

~ Chris Gardner

CHAPTER 5:

See the world as it really is… NOT THE WAY YOU WANT IT TO BE

•••••

Your ability to generate success in the job interview process is only as good as your ability to be ruthlessly realistic and strategize based on that reality…

Let me be as clear as possible: this chapter has absolutely NOTHING to do with changing who you are for the purpose of getting hired. I personally do not believe that you should change who you are for a job. Doing so will neither help you or the organization that you're applying to. Trying to change yourself for the sake of getting a job will only rob you of your authenticity, and therefore negatively impact your application of the concepts, techniques, and strategies that I'm sharing with you in this book. I NEVER want you to CHANGE yourself for the job interview process, but I ALWAYS want you to ENHANCE yourself based on having a ruthlessly realistic perspective about who you are, the value you bring, and the employment situation that is in front of you.

In many areas of life, having a "realistic" mindset might actually hinder you from accomplishing your goals. Luckily, that's just not the case in the job interview process. When you want to get hired at a job that you're interested in, you must practice seeing the world as it really is prior to you even submitting your resume. See, the job interview process is a lot like playing chess. You have to see the board as it really is, and then do your best to think at least 2-5 steps ahead so you don't end up taking actions that could get your king captured. With job hunting, you have to be proactive so that you won't do anything to either cancel you out of consideration or come back to haunt you later on.

One thing that I typically do, and I've trained other candidates to do, is a realism exercise prior to applying for any job. The purpose of this exercise is to help you take a realistic assessment of your compatibility with a job. This exercise is powerful because it will force you to identify your strengths and weaknesses prior to potentially wasting anyone's time. It will also help you start thinking of some of the ways that you can potentially overcome weaknesses that you may have by creating strategies.

The exercise is a piece of cake. All you have to do is print off a copy of the job description of the role you're interested in and start asking yourself a series of questions about your alignment with the role you're interested in. Start by making an affirmative statement based on the requirements articulated on the job description, and then ask yourself if your background is in alignment. Here are some examples of questions that you might ask yourself prior to officially applying for a job:

- This position requires 10 years of sales experience, so do I have 10 years of sales experience?

- This role is located in Baltimore, MD, and I'm based in Atlanta, GA. Would I be willing to relocate for this role?

- This role requires at least 5 years experience in IT sales. Do I have any experience in selling IT products, services and/or solutions, and have I done so for the last 5 years?

- This role requires me to have an MBA. Do I have an MBA?
- I think you get the point...

I know this may seem a little elementary, but I personally do this exercise for any and every job that I apply for. I do it because, like I mentioned previously, I want to do everything possible to increase my odds of getting hired. I don't want to lie, embellish, exaggerate, stretch the truth, etc. If I apply for a job, I want to make sure that I've taken a very realistic assessment of my background and its alignment with the role prior to applying.

The example above is just one example of seeing the world as it really is. There are many more examples I could use throughout the job interview process. This concept applies to each and every step in the process. You have to force yourself to see the world as it really is, and not the way you want it to be.

Imagine that your goal was to climb to the top of Mt. Everest. You wake up one day, and instead of planning and trying to figure out the most effective way to overcome potential obstacles, you decide that you're going to just strikeout and accomplish your goal. You look at the very top of Mount Everest and begin embarking on your journey. Now let's say that you decide that you're going to keep your eyes focused on the top of Mount Everest the entire time you're climbing. You don't ever take your eyes off the top of the mountain; you just focus there and trust that everything is going to work out. What do you think the odds are that you're going to make it to the top?

If I were a betting man, I would likely say that your odds wouldn't be very high for making it to the top of the mountain. Why? By keeping your eyes laser-focused on the top of the mountain, you're not able to see the world as it really is. You're so focused on a future result, that you're missing all the critical steps that are right in front of you that must be successfully overcome if you ever expect to get to the top of the mountain. See, that's how many people go through the job interview process. They focus so much on getting the job that they neglect the steps to get there. You as a candidate have the responsibility of creating the very best perception possible for yourself at every level of the job interview process. If you focus on your potential results too much, then you'll never focus on the reality of your current situation and thus, you'll never be able to create strategies for overcoming the real challenges that are in front of you in the job interview process which are covered later in this book.

"YOU ARE THE ONLY PERSON WHO CAN TAKE YOU WHERE YOU WANT TO GO. THERE IS NO GURU, TEACHER, MENTOR, AUTHOR, SPEAKER, SHAMAN, OR WHATEVER WHO CAN OR WILL DO THAT FOR YOU"

~ Frank Kern

CHAPTER 6:

Destroying Competition... LEAD WITH VALUE & EXCEED WITH VALUE

•••••

The easiest way to eliminate the majority of your competition is to destroy them with the value you contribute...

There's another marketing professional named Frank Kern that I also would consider to be my mentor. Although I've never actually met Frank personally, I have learned so much about effectively marketing and selling my ideas to other people from him. One of the most valuable concepts that I've learned from him was about eliminating competition. It's a concept that he calls "results in advance", but for the purpose of this book, I've decided to call it lead with value and exceed with value.

Frank's philosophy on this subject is very simple: there are 3 ways that you can go about establishing credibility and eliminating competition.

1. You can tell people how great you are at solving problems.

2. You can have someone else tell people how great you are at solving problems.

3. You can demonstrate how great you are at solving problems by actually solving them in advance.

All three of these approaches definitely work. There are plenty of people that boldly go out into the world and tell people how great they are without actually showing documentable proof of their statements, and it still works. There are also plenty of people that rely on the strong referrals from other people to establish credibility and eliminate competition. There is also a rare class of individual that doesn't focus on the top two ways of establishing credibility and eliminating competition. This person focuses on demonstrating how great they are by actually delivering results in advance.

When Frank broke this down to me, I knew instantly that group 3 is definitely where I wanted to be. In anything I do, whether we're talking about my occupation of being an executive recruiter or whether we're talking about going through an interview process, I'm always trying to figure out the things I can do to give myself the competitive advantage and absolutely destroy my competition. Ethically of course! After learning this valuable information, the first thing that popped in my mind was to "lead with value and exceed with value". I decided that giving as much value as possible up front was going to be my competitive advantage. I also decided that looking for every way possible to give exponential value at every step of any consideration process was going to be my way of creating distance from any competition that I was facing in that moment.

So, how does this "lead with value and exceed with value" philosophy apply to the job interview process? As mentioned in a previous chapter, the competition in the employment market is already fierce, and it's not going to do anything but increase as time goes on due to technological advancements. Leading with value is going to help you get noticed by potential employers. Like I mentioned previously, if you want to lead with value, then one of the first things you can focus on before you apply for a job is ask yourself the following question: what is one problem that I can help a company solve?

As an example, if I wanted to "lead with value" with a potential employer *(as a sales professional)*, I would start out by doing some research on the company. I would try to find out what their sales group did in revenue last year. Let's say that I was able to confirm that the hiring manager's sales group did approximately $3 million in sales last year. I know that any good hiring manager is always focused on finding ways to increase sales. So, I might approach this hiring manager by saying something like, " Hi {Hiring Manager Name}, I'm reaching out to you because I was hoping that I might be able to schedule about 20-30 minutes on your calendar to show you a detailed plan that I have created to help you increase your sales by $1 million dollars over the next 12 months by being in your open sales consultant position. Would you be open scheduling some time to discuss this plan?"

In the example above, I'm reaching out to a hiring manager because I'm interested in getting a job as a sales consultant on his/her team. I'm not telling this hiring manager how awesome I am. I'm not telling this hiring manager to talk to someone else so that person can brag about how great I am. Don't get me wrong: both of those approaches could potentially work. I'm basically applying the "lead with value" philosophy by asking this hiring manager for his/her time so I can DEMONSTRATE that I can help him or her dramatically increase sales by showing him/her a detailed plan for doing so. See, if this hiring manager is serious about increasing sales, the first problem this person would have to solve is figuring out a realistic plan of how to do so. If as a candidate, I'm helping solve their problems by bringing a detailed plan to the table FOR FREE, don't you think this will instantly help me get my foot in the door with the hiring manager's employment opportunity? More than likely, the answer would be yes!

Once you've led with value and been able to successfully acquire the full attention of the hiring manager, then you want to focus on exceeding with value! You exceed with value by looking for every possible opportunity to *add* value at every step of the job interview process. Here is a list of ways that you might be able to add value at various parts of the job interview process:

- Be very responsive to requests
- Maintain a positive *(can do)* attitude at all times
- Dress very professional when you show up to a face-to-face interview
- Make sure that your personal hygiene is appropriate for an interview
- Bring extra copies of your resume on professional paper to your interview
- Have manners
- Be pleasantly authentic to every person that you interact with at the company

At this point you might be thinking to yourself, "Most of the things listed above are common sense things". If that's what you're thinking, then I agree with you! There are tons and tons of people who neglect to use some of these common-sense approaches to exceed with value in the job interview process. As an executive recruiter, I've seen brilliant and extremely skillful candidates that have blown it for themselves in the interview process because, for one reason or another, they did not execute some of these common-sense things that are perceived as extremely valuable to hiring professionals.

Later in this book, you'll be learning about specific strategies that you can execute to effectively lead with value and exceed with value in much greater detail. For now, I just want you to understand that you can blow the majority of your competition away by simply executing this philosophy. The reality of the matter is that you will always have tons of competition regardless of what job you're applying for, but if you focus on leading with value and exceeding with value, it will be very easy to destroy the overwhelming majority of your competition that you'll be facing in the job interview process.

"THE ONLY THINGS IN THIS LIFE THAT YOU'LL REALLY REGRET ARE THE RISKS – AND ADVENTURES – YOU DIDN'T TAKE."

~ Dan Pena

CHAPTER 7:

You must be prepared to KISS A LOT OF FROGS

•••••

In order for your employment dreams to come true, you must be willing to become desensitized to failure…

It doesn't matter how smart, well connected, or qualified you are… You typically cannot escape failure. Even if you're the best candidate in the world, at the very least, you're going to have to expose yourself to possible failure in order to progress forward in your career and in life in general. Even if you're a great candidate, all types of things could change in the middle of your consideration process that could cause you to fail at landing the job of your dreams. Here are a few things, which you have no control over, that could potentially happen and cause you to fail in the job interview process:

- The company could decide to place a moratorium on all hiring activities for any number of reasons
- A better candidate could have entered the process, which causes them to halt all activities to focus on getting that other candidate.
- The hiring manager might love your background, but someone else in the hiring process may not be as big of a fan.

Sometimes things can happen in the middle of you being considered for a position that will cause you not to get the job. Oftentimes when these things happen, as a candidate, you'll never know about it because no one will ever tell you. You will typically not get this feedback because the company doesn't want to give you ammunition that you could use against them in a lawsuit. You know as well as I do that we live in a very litigious society nowadays.

Knowing that most of the time you're not going to really know why you're not being considered, the most important thing you can do is always stay laser-focused on controlling the controllables. There are many things that you can control in the job interview process, but for the sake of this chapter, I want you to constantly focus on generating new opportunities for yourself. The more opportunities that you're able to generate for yourself, the less pressure you will feel if things do not work out for one reason or another.

I'm sure that we all know that generating more opportunities is a common-sense way to increase your odds of landing a great job, so why don't more people focus on generating more opportunities when there is nothing stopping them from doing so? In my opinion, most people are afraid of rejection and disappointment. They would rather avoid taking actions to generate opportunities, than to be shot down. But like the 50 Billion Dollar Man (Dan Pena) once said, "You got to be willing to kiss a lot of frogs if you want to be successful".

Dan Pena is an extremely successful businessman that has helped many business professionals--including Gov. Rick Scott of Florida--successfully raise capital and grow their businesses. Once in a seminar, he mentioned this concept of kissing a lot of frogs. He was with a friend of his that mentioned to him that hooking up with people is like kissing a lot of frogs. If you were willing to put your fear aside and execute this unpleasant activity, you would eventually win because it's always a game of numbers. Dan went on to tell a story about how his friend got out of the limo in the middle of New York and started approaching every beautiful woman that passed by to ask them out. He mentioned that he saw his friend get spit on, slapped, cursed out, and everything else you can imagine. Somewhere close to the 20th woman he approached, his friend got lucky. She was interested in this guy and got in the car with him to go out on the spot.

The reason I'm telling you the "G-rated" version of this story that Dan Pena spoke about is because I want you to understand that it will likely require you to embrace this type of mentality to find the right employment opportunity for you. There are no guarantees in the job interview process, and it is your 100% personal responsibility to create as many employment opportunities for yourself that is needed to increase your odds of success. You cannot allow your fear of the word "NO", and all of its variations, to cause you to miss out on the right opportunity for you. I've oftentimes told people that the word "NO" has killed more dreams than the plague. You must become desensitized to failure. You must be willing to kiss a lot of frogs to make your employment dreams come true.

Always remember this when it comes to kissing a lot of frogs in the job interview process: you can always ask for what you want, regardless of how crazy it may seem. Never allow yourself to compromise! When I'm maneuvering through the job interview process personally, I always focus on engaging as many opportunities as I possibly can. I focus on maintaining a mindset of kissing a lot of frogs even once I've gotten in the job interview process. I always ask for what I want. Typically, I will take a three-step solution process when it comes to kissing a lot of frogs.

1. I think bigger

2. I ask for the moon

3. I say less to more people

    If you're going to kiss a lot of frogs in order to make your employment aspirations come true, don't allow yourself to compromise. Start by thinking bigger than where you are. Don't be afraid to pursue opportunities that seem slightly out of reach. Don't be afraid to ask for the moon. If you're going to run the chance of someone saying no anyways, you might as well ask for what your really want! Lastly, I would recommend that you say less to more people. I actually get this saying from a very successful network marketer named Ray Higdon. There is no magical way of asking for what you want, so your best bet is to get to the point and ask for what you really want in the fastest possible way in order to get your answer fast and move on if someone is not interested. I use this approach when I'm kissing a lot of frogs in the job interview process, and I believe these concepts might be helpful for you as well.

"ENVY IS IGNORANCE, IMITATION IS SUICIDE."

~ Ralph Waldo Emerson

CHAPTER 8:

You must learn how to be THE PURPLE ZEBRA

•••••

The world is constantly going to desire for you to fit in... But in order to be successful in the job interview process, it's all about STANDING OUT...

From a candidate's perspective, one of the most difficult tasks that you will have to accomplish if you want to land the job of your dreams is drawing attention to yourself. You can be a phenomenal candidate for an employment opportunity, but if the hiring professionals never find you then you'll never have a chance to get that job! It is your responsibility to make sure that you do everything possible to get on the radar of the hiring manager's mind that you're looking to work for. You cannot leave this extremely vital part of the process up to chance like most candidates do. There is way too much competition in the job interview process to sit back and hope that a hiring manager is going to find you. They might find you, but more than likely they won't if you sit back and hope.

Your ability to get attention from the very beginning to the very end is going to be absolutely vital to your success in the job interview process. Getting attention is important because it is all about overcoming obscurity. Obscurity is defined as the state of being unknown, inconspicuous, or unimportant. You must understand that there are three different levels to obscurity that you must overcome in the employment process in order to get the type of attention that you need to land your dream job.

1st Level of Obscurity: *They don't know you exist…*

As I mentioned before, in the job interview process, it is your responsibility to do whatever is necessary in order to become a blip on the hiring manager's radar. If you never get the hiring manager's attention, then you'll never become a blip on his/her radar. If you never become a blip on the hiring manager's radar, then you'll never even have the chance to be in consideration for the role that you're interested in. There's a 100% chance that a hiring manager will never hire you if you never get his/her initial attention.

2nd Level of Obscurity: *They don't know your value…*

Let's imagine for a second that you were able to get the initial attention of the hiring manager. If that hiring manager isn't clear of the potential value that you can bring to the table, then he or she will not remain interested in maintaining their attention on you. We've all heard the expression before, "It's not about what you know, it's about who you know". In my opinion, that's just not true; especially in the job interview process. If you want to get someone's attention, you have to first become a blip on their radar, then quickly follow that up by helping them understand the potential value that you bring to the table. That's the only way that you'll keep their attention after the initial meeting.

3rd **Level of Obscurity: You're not staying on the top level of their mind…**

Once you've initially captured the attention of a hiring manager, and you've successfully maintained their attention by showing your value, then it's time for you to focus on staying on top of their mind. The third level of obscurity is actually the most valuable level. In an ideal situation, you would want to create omnipresence in the job interview process. Omnipresence is defined as the state of being widespread or constantly encountered. Omnipresence in the job interview process should be your goal because there are many distractions that a hiring manager can potentially be dealing with while they're considering hiring you. If you can successfully stay in the forefront of the Hiring Manager's mind, that can oftentimes end up causing the hiring manager to think positively about you and potentially cause them to feel confident about your candidacy for the career opportunity.

Now that you understand the three levels of obscurity that you must overcome if you want to successfully get and maintain the attention of a hiring manager, I want you to understand why it is so important to get this attention. Most people have been raised to be quiet and avoid getting attention. Most of the time, your mom, dad, or provider probably told you to be quiet and don't draw attention to yourself. While that training may have helped your parents, it doesn't do very much by the way of helping you when you become working age. If you don't get attention *(and maintain attention)* in the job interview process, you won't get a job. Plain and simple.

You have to learn how to be the purple zebra in the flock of zebras! According to Glassdoor, the average job opening attracts 250 resumes! To some people, 250 might not sound like a lot of people, but let me ask you this. Have you ever tried speaking to 250 people at one time *(during a speech)* about the same thing? I would argue that most have never spoken to 250 people before, but I have. I can tell you from first hand experience that 250 people is a lot! Imagine being a hiring manager and having to be responsible for your day-to-day responsibilities, and then you have to find someone out of 250+ resumes to hire for the position you have available on your team. That many resumes would likely look like a flock of zebras, and it would likely be very difficult for you to make a decision.

When you decide that you're interested in being considered for any job, you need to understand that you're essentially going to be forced to look like a zebra in the beginning. It is your responsibility to acquire and maintain the attention of the hiring manager amongst all of that other competition that's applying for the same job and making the process noisier. By applying the principles, concepts, techniques and strategies shared with you in this book, you'll have the power to change your color from black and white to full blown purple. You'll have the ability to make it 10 times easier for a hiring manager to notice you and want to consider you for his/her opportunity. Due to your willingness to stand out, you'll exponentially increase the likelihood of being selected as the ideal candidate of choice.

"NO MATTER HOW TALENTED YOU ARE, YOUR TALENT WILL FAIL YOU, IF YOU'RE NOT SKILLED. SKILL IS ACHIEVED THROUGH PRACTICE. WORK HARD AND DEDICATE YOURSELF TO BEING BETTER EVERY SINGLE DAY"

~ Will Smith

CHAPTER 9:

BE DISCIPLINED IN THIS WORLD, or be disciplined by this world

• • • • •

If you want to have a better life from an employment perspective, you must choose to be ruthlessly disciplined about executing what's necessary in order to improve your employment situation...

The difference between bad and average is a decision. The difference between average and good is skill. But the difference between good and great is discipline! Without discipline, a person can never accomplish greatness in anything-- much less in the job interview process. Discipline is defined as the practice of training people to obey rules or a code of behavior. The people who accomplish the most in life are those who do not rely on others to train them, but rather focus on learning what's necessary so they can train themselves. The "greats" in any arena execute a high level of personal responsibility and take it upon themselves to track down the best information. Then, they execute a high level of discipline to train until they get the results that they desire.

In order to dramatically improve your employment skills, you're going to have to embrace a mindset of discipline. If you want to dramatically improve your career and start reaping the rewards that you desire, you're going to have to be disciplined when it comes to improving every aspect of your employment skills. Although employment skills are vital when it comes to getting a job, employment skills are equally as important when it comes to keeping a job and continuing to progress your career. You must have the discipline to learn and execute repeatedly until these employment skills become second nature.

I want to make sure that your expectations are managed properly. The skills that you're going to learn in this book are practical and simple, but please don't mistake them for being easy. That's why I'm trying to emphasize the importance of discipline to you. If you're not willing to be disciplined enough to sit down and learn these ideas, strategies, and concepts, then you're definitely not going to be disciplined enough to execute. Your career success is going to be directly proportional to the amount of discipline you choose to execute in its improvement. You need to be aware that there are no shortcuts to this! Success in the job interview process is totally feasible if you're willing to be disciplined, but you must be willing to pay the price for the success you desire.

One of the biggest mistakes that I see a lot of people make in many areas of life, especially in the job interview process, is that they tend to look at extremely skillful people and think that somehow those people are winning in life because they got lucky or caught a big break. People who tend to believe these falsehoods usually never take the time to truly analyze how much hard work, dedication, and, most importantly, discipline it took these so-called "lucky" people to make their skills come across as lucky. These "lucky" people have probably invested countless hours in developing their craft, and they've probably experienced much more rejection and failure than most people are aware of. But through it all, they remained disciplined!

Whenever I think about discipline and skill, I always think about the Kobe Bryant and Bow Wow situation. Just in case you're not familiar, Kobe Bryant and Bow Wow happened to be in the same gym together. I'm not exactly sure what Bow Wow was thinking on this particular day, but he decided that he was going to test Kobe Bryant-- (a man who has been dedicated and disciplined to his craft for decades.) Bow Wow decided that he was going to challenge and bet Kobe Bryant that he could get to 10 points before Kobe in a one-on-one game. MISTAKE! Kobe gladly accepted that bet, and was even nice enough to give Bow Wow nine points to start the game! That's right. Bow Wow only had to score one basket and he would have won. He would have been able to tell everybody that he won his bet and beat one of the greatest basketball players ever.

Things didn't quite go as planned for Bow Wow. He attempted to score on Kobe Bryant, and he failed. As you can probably imagine, after Kobe got the ball, he completely dominated the rest of the game. Somewhere around Kobe's 5th or 6th basket, he told Bow Wow something that goes down in my book as being one of my favorite quotes of all time. Kobe said, "There's a big difference between seeing the sharks on the discovery channel and being out in the water with them, huh!" You see, Bow Wow made the huge mistake of thinking that he could compete with someone as skilled as Kobe Bryant. Although it was all fun and games, Bow Wow should have never tested Kobe Bryant, much less, challenged him to a one-on-one game. Bow Wow was completely out of his league and didn't stand a chance from the very beginning because Kobe Bryant's skills were far too advanced. Bow Wow wasn't even close to being competition.

What does this have to do with discipline and the job interview process? Every day there are people that are trying to apply for jobs to enhance their employment situations, but they don't realize that they're destined for failure before they ever get started. They want to have the great employment results without ever paying the price and becoming disciplined about improving their employment skills. Now that you have this book, you'll have access to the knowledge that you need in order to dominate in the job interview process just like Kobe dominated against Bow Wow in that game. Your competition will never stand a chance!

When you embrace the information in this book and then have the discipline to actually execute upon this information, you'll have the skills necessary to take control of your employment destiny. You'll no longer have to leave your success in the job interview process up to hope and chance. By disciplining yourself to learn this information and execute this information, you can transition from building someone else's dream to building your own. You'll be able to confidently go into any hiring situation knowing that you have the skills to handle anything because you are focused on getting disciplined and remaining disciplined until your skills became second nature to you. That's the power of being disciplined!

"SOME DAYS ARE HARDER THAN OTHERS TO GET UP EARLY & GRIND, BUT I'D MUCH RATHER SUFFER A LITTLE TODAY THAN STRUGGLE THE REST OF MY LIFE!"

~ Eric Thomas (ET)

CHAPTER 10:

LIONS & GAZELLES… Embrace the path of unreasonable action

•••••

Your willingness to take unreasonable action towards accomplishing your goals, is the closest you'll ever get to guaranteed success…

Your success in the job interview process will be largely dependant upon your willingness to get up every day and take massive action towards accomplishing your employment goals. I'll never forget watching a television show where Steve Harvey gave the best analogy I've ever heard about the importance of taking massive action each day. Steve said, "Every morning in Africa, a gazelle wakes up. It knows it must outrun the fastest lion or it will be killed. Every morning in Africa, a lion wakes up. It knows it must run faster than the slowest gazelle or it will starve. It doesn't matter whether you're the lion or gazelle – when the sun comes up, you'd better be running!"

Steve Harvey was telling this lesson because he was trying to articulate the importance of waking up every day and taking massive action. When you're going through the job interview process, the greatest competitive advantage that you'll ever have is the willingness to take unreasonable amounts of action towards landing your dream job. The great news is that it actually doesn't take much action to get to the land of unreasonable. Most people approach the employment process with a mindset of doing the least possible amount of activity to get the job. When you're going against competition that has this type of mindset, you only need to do a little bit more to beat them out. Your goal should be to take so much action in the job interview process that you dominate the thought process of the hiring manager.

Thinking about the power of unreasonable action makes me think about a very special candidate that I worked with in the job interview process quite some time ago: my wife! I remember her situation like it was yesterday. She was working for a very large insurance organization, and she was pretty satisfied with her job at that time. She came home one day and told me that some of the higher ups called a meeting with all the employees and mentioned that corporate was thinking about potentially moving her office from one state to another. She told me that they hadn't made up their minds yet, but they were considering the move as an option. I politely informed her that they were *definitely* going to move the office! I told her that the leadership at her company would have never made that type of announcement if they hadn't already made their mind up that they were going to make that transition.

As predicted, this company eventually ended up notifying her and others that they were officially going to move locations. They could care less that she was one of the strongest workers that they had. They had made their decision, and that was that. They gave her a very simple choice: move to this next location and keep her job or stay where she was, and they would thank her for her service. She chose the latter and began her job search.

She started applying to quite a few jobs. Because she has a strong background, she was able to successfully schedule several face-to-face interviews, but many of those interviews didn't work out for one reason or another. She eventually started to get frustrated and asked me for my help so she could do better in her interviews. My wife is phenomenal when it comes to her craft, but like most professionals, she's not a professional interviewer.

After she asked for help, I started coaching her on things she could do during the interview that would help her exponentially increase her odds. The very first company that she ended up implementing these tactics with was the company that ended up hiring her. However, it totally wasn't as easy as it might sound. Many of the tactics that I taught her to do in the actual interview process required her to take action that most people never take. She took that action, and her interview went by smoothly.

After the interview, she called me, and I urged her to take several actions that most people would likely say is unreasonable. In fact, even *she* thought one of the things I told her to do was completely unreasonable. I told her to write a thank you letter, print it off on nice paper, sign it, and then send it to the hiring manager using the most expensive mailing service she could buy that would guarantee that this Hiring Manager would receive the mail the very next morning. My wife is pretty frugal, so she definitely thought this was a completely unnecessary task. Reluctantly, she decided to listen to me and do what I asked her to do. Here's the best part: she *didn't* end up getting that job!

As you probably guessed, she wasn't necessarily a happy camper after she did all the EXTRA stuff that ended up leading her nowhere.

Thankfully, she eventually got over it and started back going through her job search. After a couple of weeks of applying to jobs without having any success at setting up interviews, she noticed that that same company that rejected her ended up having another role that she thought might be in better alignment with her background. She ended up applying for that role and eventually brought in for another interview. This time, her interview experience was vastly different than the last time.

When she went in for this interview, she happened to walk past the hiring manager that originally shot her down. The hiring manager instantly recognized her. She thanked my wife for sending that letter *(which by the way, no candidate had ever done)*, and then she got up and walked to the new hiring manager for this new position and told him that he needed to hire her for his role. My wife sat down for the job interview, and the hiring manager didn't ask her a single interview question. They literally sat there and just talked about random things for almost an hour.

After leaving the interview, she was understandably very confused at the exchange. She called me and told me what happened and said that she doesn't know what to think. I told her that this was an *awesome* sign! All that unreasonable action that she took the first time around is paying dividends as we speak. In the middle of my wife continuing to explain this interesting interviewing experience, she received a call from the company's HR department. To make a long story not as long, she ended up being offered the job and taking home much more than she was making at her previous company.

I tell you this story to help you understand the significance of "unreasonable actions" in the job interview process. Most people that go through the process are either too lazy or too scared to take unreasonable action. Their laziness and fear make your job ten-times easier. If you're simply willing to take more action towards showing your value in the job interview process than everyone else, you put yourself in a very favorable position. You might not be guaranteed to get the job, but you'll have a much better chance at creating a lasting impression on potential hiring managers. Everyone wants to feel wanted, and there's no better way to make a hiring manager feel special than by showing him/her that you're willing to take unreasonable action to prove that you truly appreciate their time and want to help them solve their problems.

PART 2: Mastering The Outer Game Of Employment Success

"SIMPLICITY IS THE ULTIMATE SOPHISTICATION"

~ Leonardo de Vinci

CHAPTER 11:

It's not ROCKET SCIENCE, but it is a science

• • • • •

People who have great job interview skills never have to rely on hope...

Unfortunately, most people have never received training on how to effectively maneuver the job interview process. This statement reigns true regardless of background, race, title, creed, socio-economic status, etc. Most people have never been trained on how to go into a cold job marketplace and successfully generate employment opportunities for themselves. Those who have received some type of employment training from school, parents, or friends typically have been taught what I like to refer to as zebra employment training. They've learned how to do the exact same things that everybody else in the job market is doing. As a result, they usually end up looking like a zebra in a pack of zebras. Although I wouldn't dare say that the job interview process is easy, I would say that this particular strategy in itself is a very simple one. If you're willing to apply yourself, you can end up exponentially increasing your odds for success.

The great news is that going through the job interview process is a lot like baking a cake from scratch. When you want to bake a cake from scratch, you have to start by first identifying all the necessary ingredients that you'll need to get the final product. Once you've identified all the ingredients that you need, you can't just randomly throw the ingredients together and think that you're going to come out with the ideal final product. You have to figure out how much of each ingredient you need, then mix them together in a very specific order. If not, you'll potentially throw off the whole recipe. Then once you've mixed everything together in the right order and measurements, you can't just throw it in your oven at whatever temperature you want. You have to figure out what the right temperature is for your recipe and ensure that it's cooked properly.

Do you see the science woven in this analogy? When you're going through the job interview process, while you can't control the ultimate outcome of any given opportunity, you need to understand that there is a science to exponentially increasing your odds for success. Throughout the remainder of this book, I'm going to literally walk you step-by-step through the entire job interview process and share with you some ideas (aka recipes) that you can use to give yourself a competitive advantage. You don't need to freestyle or wing-it. You just need to gain understanding of the practical ideas that I'll be sharing with you and use what you see fit to help you get better results and increase your odds.

What you're about to learn in this part of the book is the science behind increasing your odds at every level of the job interview process. I'm currently a Headhunter (aka Executive Recruiter) by occupation, and whenever I work with a candidate to help him/her maneuver through this process, I'm laser-focused on helping them increase their odds at every step of the way. The starting point of increasing your odds in the job interview process is by understanding that there are six independent and unique phases that you must successfully overcome if you want to land that big job.

- PHASE I: Performing Strategic Recon
- PHASE II: Becoming The Ideal Blip
- PHASE III: Painting The Mona Lisa
- PHASE IV: Creating A Sense Of Certainty
- PHASE V: The Magic Is In The Follow-Up
- PHASE VI: How To Get What You Really Want

Having a firm grasp on these six phases will pretty much serve as your roadmap for success. Similar to the example that I gave you earlier about baking a cake, you need to understand that these six phases are in this order for a reason. While you're definitely free to approach this process how you see fit, you must also understand that each phase has a unique purpose that feeds into the next phase. Ultimately, each feeds into the desired outcome of being the ideal candidate that is selected for the opportunity that you're interested in.

Learn how to master these six phases and watch how your confidence in the job interview process will start to fly through the roof. No longer will you be second-guessing yourself. No longer will you find yourself in a reactive mindset where things are just happening to you in this process. From this point forward, you'll be in a position to take proactive steps towards controlling your destiny. While your competition is busy doing what everyone else is doing and winging it throughout the majority of the job interview process, you'll be in a position to take skillful action at every step which will help you differentiate yourself and gain an immense competitive advantage over the other zebras. Oops... I mean candidates.

> **"EVERY BATTLE IS WON BEFORE IT IS FOUGHT"**
>
> ~ Sun Tzu

CHAPTER 12:

Performing STRATEGIC RECON

• • • • •

Your success in the job interview process should never boil down to hope, luck or coincidence. Every action you take in this process should be with the expressed intention of increasing your odds. The starting place of increasing your odds is having a strategic plan for success prior to taking any action towards the accomplishment of your goal...

WRITE THE VISION DOWN AND MAKE IT PLAIN

THE UGLY TRUTH (T.U.T) ACTION STEP #1: Write down your five-year career goal from an industry perspective, and then write down the first logical career step towards achieving that goal.

Easily one of the biggest mistakes that I see people make when starting out in the job interview process is that they only think about the situation that they're currently in, and they don't take any time to think about what the future will look like. Regardless of what job you end up pursuing in the near future, it's going to take a lot of time and effort to successfully go through the job hiring process to land the job. If you're going to invest the time and energy into getting a job, you should begin your search by focusing on jobs in an industry that truly align with what you're trying to accomplish long-term.

Let me give you an example of the importance of this… My current occupation is that of a Headhunter *(aka Executive Recruiter)*. Prior to working in this industry, I had absolutely no experience in recruiting. Before landing this job, I was in a difficult financial crunch, but I still thought out my long-term goals. I didn't allow my need for money to cause me to compromise on getting into the industry that I was truly interested in. I had previously helped many people find and land their dream jobs before recruiting, so I figured that recruiting would be a field that I would be genuinely interested in. I thought about what I wanted my career life to look like within 5 years, and I determined that I wanted to be a top producer in the recruiting industry.

As a result of thinking out this five-year goal, I was able to cater my search efforts for a recruiting opportunity that would be in alignment with my background. I wasn't just randomly applying to every job in the market hoping that someone would hire me. I was able to find an opportunity that was in pretty strong alignment with my background and ultimately end up landing a Headhunter role. Just like I set my five-year goal to give me direction in my search, I want you to do the same. You're going to have to work hard to get a job anyway, so you might as well make sure that you're focusing on work that you wouldn't mind doing on a long-term basis.

SOCIAL MEDIA… THE GIFT OR THE CURSE

T.U.T ACTION STEP #2: Perform a detailed social media audit of ALL of your accounts. Perception is everything, so if it doesn't 100% show you in a positive light, then you need to delete it or shut your account down completely.

Social media can be the biggest gift to you in the job interview process or it can be the biggest curse. You have to understand something very important about social media... As a human being that has free access to setting up social media accounts, you have the "right" to post whatever content your heart desires. Nobody *(including me or anyone else)* has the "right" to tell you what you can or cannot post. After all, it is *your* account! BUT, with that being said, you must also understand that everyone else has the "right" to think and perceive whatever they'd like about the content that you chose to post. Whether someone hates or loves the content you share, you're going to have to live with those consequences either way.

My recommendation would be to do a detailed and BRUTALLY HONEST audit and assessment of all of your social media accounts BEFORE you ever apply for a single job. I would even find someone that you respect from a professional perspective and ask them to go through your social media accounts and offer you honest feedback. If you or anyone else identifies content that you've posted that is unprofessional in any way, I would recommend that you either delete that post or temporarily shut down your account until you've successfully landed the job. This is one area where you would rather be safe than sorry!

I know this might seem a little excessive, but I assure you that it is absolutely necessary. I can't even begin to tell you how many times I've seen people get rejected for jobs over something petty on their social media account. You know what the worst part is? What the ugly truth is? If I had to guess, I would imagine that easily over 95% of people were passed up for a job because of something seemingly inappropriate that was posted on their social media account. They never had the slightest clue that they missed out on the job because of something typed on a screen. I tell candidates all the time that these companies are not interested in training you how to get a job. They expect you to present yourself in a certain manner, or they have absolutely no problem passing on you!

I'll never forget this interesting situation that happened at one of my previous jobs. This company had an open position that they were looking to fill. As you can probably imagine, they posted the job and all of a sudden, they started getting a flood of resumes. The Hiring Decision Maker (HDM) ended up coming across this one particular candidate's resume and was excited about potentially speaking to her. The HDM decided to do a quick search on Facebook for the candidate, and instantly got turned off. The HDM went to her Facebook account and saw that her profile picture was of her in a bathing suit drinking a glass of alcohol.

The HDM noticed that the candidate had graduated from my college, so the HDM came up to me and asked me if I knew her. I told the HDM that I didn't know her, and the next words out of her mouth were words I'll never forget. She said, "You may want to reach out to this candidate and let her know that thousands of dollars were lost because of one unprofessional picture." Because I didn't know her, I wasn't going to go through the trouble of reaching out to make her aware of this feedback. Nonetheless, I'll never forget those words, and neither should you. It may not be fair, but this is the real world! This is happening every day. Every day there are people that are missing out on great opportunities because of their social media accounts. Don't you end up being one of those people!

THE RIGHT JOBS… CHOOSE YOUR GENUINE INTEREST

T.U.T ACTION STEP #3: Search and create a list of five ideal career opportunities, then print off the job descriptions.

Now that you've written down your 5-year vision and listed the first logical career step to accomplishing your vision, you need to focus on identifying jobs that are in alignment with your first logical career step. You want to make sure that you find at least five opportunities to focus on. Five is a good number because you don't want to put all of your eggs in one basket. Marketing genius Dan Kennedy once mentioned, "the worst number in all of business is the number one." The point that Dan was trying to make is that (in business) you never want to rely on one client, one product, or one marketing approach. By focusing on one of anything, you make yourself very vulnerable for failure. That same sentiment definitely applies in the employment process. You want to make sure that you have multiple opportunities that you're working so you can increase your odds of having success.

Thankfully, you have many options for finding the five opportunities that you need to identify. Prior to the Internet, you only had a few different ways that you could go about uncovering potential opportunities, but now there are many different resources. Below, I've listed some of the resources that you can use to identify potential job opportunities:

- Internet Job Boards (Indeed, Career Builder, Monster, etc.)
- Company websites
- Referrals from friends, family and/or associates
- Job fairs
- Search Engines (Google, Yahoo, Bing, etc.)
- Editorials (Newspapers, Magazines, Newsletters, Blogs, etc.)
- Networking Events

- Social media (Linked In, Facebook, Twitter)

These are just a few ways that you can go about building your list of five potential opportunities to pursue. Please keep in mind that these are just ways that you can go about building your list based on the technology that is currently available during the time this book was written. In the future, you may have the options above, or you may have many more options at your disposal. It doesn't matter where you find the opportunity... All that matters is that you find the right opportunities somewhere.

Don't be afraid to be as creative as you'd like when it comes to identifying opportunities. You'll be surprised at some of the creative ways that you can discover great jobs. The most important thing is that you don't stop until you have successfully found five. Once you've found these opportunities, then you want to make sure that you print off the job descriptions for each job.

TARGET GRAVITATIONAL INFLUENCERS

T.U.T ACTION STEP #4: Do some research to figure out who the potential decision maker(s) are for each of your five opportunities, and track down as much of their contact information as possible. Always remember... Anyone can say NO when it comes to HIRING YOU for a job, but very few people can say YES. You want to know who the people are that can say YES, and communicate effectively with them!

What is a gravitational influencer? Thank you for asking! A gravitational influencer is any person involved in the employment decision-making process that has the authority to say yes and make things happen. Anyone, from the secretary to the CEO can say NO to hiring you, but there are very few people that actually have the authority to say YES to hiring you. While a HDM would always be considered a gravitational influencer, some situations allow room for others that could be labeled as being one as well. As an example, if you're applying for a sales job, then we know that the sales manager is likely the hiring manager, and thus would be considered a gravitational influencer. In this same example, if you decided that you wanted to reach out to the general manager or owner of that company, both of those people would be considered gravitational influencers because they have the power to say YES and make things happen in the job interview process.

The idea behind gravitational influencers is very simple. When in doubt, go as high as you can up the corporate ladder. Remember, you need to get a YES to make things happen for yourself. Then, let gravity do the rest for you. You want to know who these people are and make sure that you have as much of their contact information as you can possibly find. Your communication with these gravitational influencers is a million times more important than anyone else you'll meet during the job interview process. While you should always make it a point to be nice and respectful to everyone you meet while job hunting, you should always make it a priority to have your A-game on when attempting to communicate with these individuals.

I actually stumbled across the power of using gravitational influencers by complete accident. During my last semester in college, I had to do an internship in order to graduate. I ended up completing one with Sun Sports television network that's based out of Orlando, FL. Sun Sports was an affiliate of the Fox Network, so when I finished my internship, I always had in the back of my mind that I wanted to potentially work for either Sun Sports or Fox.

About 6-12 months after I completed my internship with Sun Sports, I noticed that the Fox Network based out of Atlanta had an account executive *or* sales person opening that I was interested in. I applied for the job through their website, and about 3 weeks went by without me hearing anything from anyone. I tried to figure out who the manager was, but at that time, LinkedIn wasn't very popular. Therefore, I couldn't figure out who the right person was that I needed to speak to. I even tried making a cold call up to Atlanta, but that wasn't helpful either. I ended up getting super frustrated and feeling like I was just spinning my wheels.

Just before I gave up all hope, I did a Google search for the Fox Network, and I happen to find a webpage for Fox that listed the top executives along with their email addresses. I thought to myself: *There's no way possible that they're crazy enough to put the email addresses of top executives on their website.* Spoiler alert ➜ I WAS WRONG. They actually had all their contact information on this webpage! There was just one little problem: the job opportunity was based out of Atlanta, and all of these executives were based out of California. I said, "What the H. E. double hockey sticks! I don't have anything to lose!" I crafted an email for the Senior Vice President and sent it to him.

What happened next was nothing short of amazing to me at that time in my life. I sent this Sr. VP *(a person I have never met by the way)* an email late in the evening, and the very next morning he responded back to me. I'll never forget that day! He wasn't mad or annoyed that I contacted him about a job that's based out of Atlanta. He thanked me for reaching out and guaranteed me that I would hear from the HDM either that day or the next day. Within 3 hours of receiving this response, I got a call from the HDM for the opportunity out of Atlanta and was interviewed for the position that

I was interested in.

I didn't end up getting the job because I just didn't have the right experience at that time; however, what I did get was a million times more valuable. I experienced what I'd like to call a paradigm shift. My previous belief was that many of these decision makers were untouchable. After that experience, I realized that if you have the wherewithal to be bold and go to the top of the org chart when trying to get a job and make a favorable impression, you can allow the gravitational force of that person's power to speed up the entire job interview process in your favor. From that day forward, I made it a common practice to identify gravitational influencers in any employment situation that I embarked on.

Back to the regular scheduled programming… You want to make sure that you have these key decision maker's contact information from the very beginning, so that you don't have to waste time scrambling to get their contact info later in the process when time is of the essence. Here is a list of some of the key details that you want to have before you ever apply for a job, if possible:

- Company website
- Decision maker name
- Decision maker email
- Decision maker phone
- Decision maker LinkedIn
- Decision maker address
- Top Executive name

- Top Executive email
- Top Executive phone
- Top Executive address
- Social media links

FIND A BIG PROBLEM & MAP OUT A BIG SOLUTION

T.U.T ACTION STEP #5: Identify a big problem that you can potentially help solve. Write down the problem and create a detailed solution to that problem so you can be prepared to speak to it if need be. You don't have to be 100% certain that your solution will work, but your solution must be thoughtful. Remember: the ONLY reason someone would ever hire someone else is to help solve a problem(s)!

As I mentioned earlier in this book, the only reason why anyone on God's green earth would hire someone is because they want to solve a problem. That's it! While every decision maker in the employment process may have a different variation of the problem that they're looking to solve, I always recommend that you take a proactive approach toward helping a potential company solve their problems. I have found that if you come to an interview with a drawn-out solution to a big problem, it typically adds a lot of value to you as a candidate.

You have to realize that most candidates' mindsets, as they're going through the job interview process, are self-centered. Essentially, they're only focused on solving their own problems. When you have a prepared solution for a potential challenge that a company may be currently facing in real time, you will immediately differentiate yourself from all the other competition. I assure you that the overwhelming majority of the people you're competing with in this job interview process are lazy and won't even think about doing something like this to get a competitive advantage.

When thinking about a problem you can help solve, you want to make sure that it is a problem that you can actually impact by being in the position that you're applying for. I'll use myself as an example, since my whole career has been focused in sales, the problem I might focus on would be increasing sales. What you don't want to do is focus on a problem where you can't impact that problem from the role that you're applying for. If I were applying for an administrative assistant job, I wouldn't focus on potentially solving a payroll problem unless I knew the company was having payroll issues and I knew that my core responsibilities would revolve around payroll issues.

Once you've found the big problem you want to address, then I want you to think creatively and create a plan for potentially addressing that problem **based on your direct actions**. When creating a potential solution to the problem, I wouldn't worry myself about being overly realistic. Just focus on being thoughtful about the different ways that you might be able to make a valuable impact by accomplishing this goal. Even if the HDM doesn't think that your solution is feasible, I assure you that your stock with that manager would have grown exponentially just by the sheer fact that you took the initiative to try and solve a big problem for them.

Now, let's assume for a minute that you just can't figure out what would be a big problem you could help solve. What do you do in that situation? Well, if I didn't know a big problem that I could address from the beginning, then I would definitely ask the HDM to tell me what big problem he/she is looking for my role to solve. Save this for the interview stage, not any time prior. This is another great question that I assure you most of your competition will not be thinking about asking.

Once you ask this question and get the response, you can take one of two approaches to build your value. You can share some ideas with the HDM about how you would potentially solve a problem of that nature, or you could follow that question up with another question that asks the HDM how he/she would approach potentially solving that big problem. Then you would reassure the HDM that you have what it takes to execute that solution. Either way, you've added a tremendous amount of value because you've articulated your interest in helping the HDM solve the problems that are important to him/her.

YOU MUST BECOME SOLD YOURSELF

T.U.T ACTION STEP #6: List 2-4 reasons per opportunity as to why you feel you would be an ideal candidate for each role. Make sure your reasons are grounded in logic and not in delusion.

This step is actually one of the most important steps in the entire job interview process! It's impossible to sell anyone else on the value you bring to a position if you're not sold yourself. Before you ever apply for a job, you should make a habit of challenging yourself as to the value that a company would receive by hiring you for a given role. As much as you may enjoy fluffing yourself up, make sure that you're realistic. The list should be based on facts and not your opinion of your abilities. If you can't make a logical case for yourself, then your time would be better served finding another opportunity that is in better alignment with your skills.

There are so many people that take a delusional approach towards getting a job. They don't care that their job experience isn't in any alignment with the role they're applying for. They're just using the "I hope" approach towards getting a job. This is a very stupid way of approaching a job search, and all they're doing is wasting both their time and the time of the potential employer. If a job description specifically states that you should have a PhD and 5 years of management experience within the Agricultural Manufacturing industry, and you have an Associates degree, with no management experience, and have only worked in the fast food industry, you're freaking delusional if you think that you stand a chance of landing that job! You have to sell yourself on a job based on the FACT that your background is legitimately in great alignment with what a HDM is looking for.

Now, let's get to the nitty gritty. Start by spreading out all five job descriptions on a table. Read each job description in detail, and try and convince yourself why you would be a good fit for each position. You should write down at least 2-4 different reasons for each opportunity. If you can't write down 2-4 logical reasons, per opportunity, as to why you would be an ideal candidate for that role, then you should seek out another opportunity where your background is in better alignment with the job duties.

Let me give you an example of how I used this strategy for the occupation I'm currently involved in as a Headhunter. Prior to the job I have at the time of writing this book, I literally had **zero experience** as a recruiter, much less executive recruiting. I always was intrigued by the idea of doing Headhunting and heard that there was good money being earned in this profession. For many years prior to getting involved in this profession, I was passionate about helping people land the jobs of their dreams and had helped many people gain employment.

I finally got to a place in my career where I was ready to try out Headhunting. When I started my job search, I came across many different types of recruiting opportunities, and I started to notice that many of the executive recruiting firms were looking for people who had previously worked as a recruiter for other firms/companies. I could have done what so many other people did and applied for the job anyway, hoping that someone might give me a shot. Instead, I decided to focus on finding an opportunity that seemed to be in good alignment with my background.

I eventually ended up finding five different recruiting opportunities that were a good fit, but one in particular seemed to be in great alignment with my background. This particular firm was offering a training program that would help someone become an executive recruiter within two years. The firm also indicated that an ideal candidate didn't have to have previous recruiting experience, but they had to have documentable success as a business developer. BINGO!

I started to make my list of logical reasons why I would be a great candidate for this opportunity well before I ever applied for the role.

Here's what I came up with…

1. I have a very strong, documentable track record as a business developer with almost a decade of success.
2. I'm a quick learner, and I have a genuine interest in learning the duties of an executive recruiter. Therefore, I would be a great candidate for a training program.
3. This job is literally within a 15-minute drive from my house, so they

wouldn't have to worry about me getting to work late, and this would be ideal for me to spend more time with my family.

Once I had this list together that was based on factual information, it was easy for me to become sold on this opportunity. Once I became sold on this opportunity, it made it 10x easier for me to have a natural enthusiasm and do the difficult activities that most candidates try to avoid. It made it easier for me to go "all-in" on my pursuit of landing this job. Once I was sold, it made it much easier to sell the hiring manager.

"THE GOAL OF A MARKETING INTERACTION ISN'T TO CLOSE THE SALE, ANY MORE THAN THE GOAL OF A FIRST DATE IS TO GET MARRIED. NO, THE OPPORTUNITY IS TO MOVE FORWARD, TO EARN ATTENTION AND TRUST AND CURIOSITY AND CONVERSATION"

~ Seth Godin

CHAPTER 13:

Becoming the IDEAL BLIP

•••••

Have you ever heard the saying, "first impressions are lasting impressions"? This motto is extremely true when it comes to the job interview process. From the very moment that you become a blip on the HDM's radar, every single detail is either going to improve your odds exponentially or decrease them.

HIGH-POWERED RIFLES vs. MACHINE GUNS... BE FOR SOMEBODY

T.U.T ACTION STEP #7: Take each job description and highlight the most important requirements of what the hiring manager has stated that he or she is looking for in an ideal candidate. The job description is like the ultimate cheat-sheet that can help you align your background to the skills and requirements that are important to that hiring authority.

Most people approach the job interview process very similar to shooting a machine gun. When you shoot a machine gun, you can pull the trigger once and fire off multiple bullets all at once. Aiming isn't nearly as important because you can randomly wave your hand and get lucky enough to hit your target. So many people do this every day when trying to get a job. They may dust off their resume a bit, but then they'll use that one resume to apply to 10, 20 or even 30+ jobs.

People that choose to use the machine gun approach will often get frustrated at the job interview process. They don't realize just how much competition they're really going against in the job market. They're using a one-size fits all approach with their resume, but there's no such thing as a one-size fits all job. Each job that you apply for is absolutely unique. This will typically even stand true if you're applying for the same job, at the same company, but in different cities. Every single job has its own set of problems and will typically have its own set of needs to solve those problems. Using a one-size fits all approach will dramatically lower your likelihood of being effective in the interview process.

On the other hand, using a high-powered rifle approach will help you exponentially increase your odds of success. When you're using a high-powered rifle approach in the interview process, every action that you take tends to be more methodical because aim becomes much more important. A high-powered rifle is designed to help you be as accurate as you possibly can be with each and every shot. Because every job situation is unique, the best way to increase your odds is to treat it as such… unique!

You want to take each of the five job descriptions that you've decided are of interest to you and look at them from a high-powered rifle approach. You want to highlight the most important features on each of those job descriptions, so you can be prepared to adapt your resume to these key areas. When highlighting important features, you want to make sure that you're highlighting the right things. You want to highlight things that are relevant to any other requirements from the job posting. Don't waste your time highlighting cliché things like "this person must have a great attitude and work well within a team environment". These are things you want to be aware of, but not necessarily things you want to highlight as important skills or requirements.

CREATE A "THANK GOD" RESUME THAT DEMANDS ATTENTION

T.U.T ACTION STEP #8: 1) Create first half excellence 2) Bullet points are your best friend 3) Make your resume keyword rich 4) Focus on numbers, skills and/or accomplishments

*** Let me start this section off with a VERY IMPORTANT WARNING. Although I DO want you to create a resume that will make a manager say "Thank God" when they finally see your background, I DON'T EVER want you to lie, exaggerate, or embellish in order to accomplish this outcome. Lying will never help you in the job interview process, or in life in general. This section is about helping you draw out the experience that you actually have in a very compelling way to make it easier for a HDM to realize that you're the ideal candidate they're looking for.

This section is all about writing a strong resume. Your resume is one of the most significant factors related to your success in the job interview process. It literally doesn't matter how skillful you are at your craft/profession. If your resume sucks, then you suck! If you're resume looks great, then you're great! Remember what I shared with you earlier in this book. In the ideal world, the person with the best skills will typically always get the job. Unfortunately, it doesn't work that way in the real world. Instead, the person that creates the best perception is going to typically get the job.

Your resume is typically the starting point of creating your perception in the mind of a hiring manager. If you don't look good on a resume, then most hiring managers won't even remotely consider you for their opportunity. If you look great on your resume, then most hiring managers will be excited and eager to meet you. You have to keep in mind that easily over 90% of the resumes that any HDM will receive for a job posting are not qualified for the role. Most people are just randomly applying to all types of jobs with the hopes that they will be miraculously selected as an ideal candidate even though their resume isn't even remotely close to the needs of the job description.

According to Ladders, the average Recruiter/HDM takes 6.25 seconds to look at a candidate's resume. While I do believe that there is some validity to this statistic, I don't think it gives you a fully accurate understanding of how this really works. In my opinion, the average is 6.25 seconds because most of the people that are submitting resumes aren't in alignment with the role. What's not being discussed is that Recruiters/HDM are spending much more time on understanding the resumes of people who actually seem to be a match for their job opening. That's why it is extremely important that you do a great job of positioning yourself well on a resume. If you're not positioned well there, then you'll never get the opportunity to position yourself well in an actual job interview.

What I'm about to share with you are a few different things that you can do to dramatically improve the impact that your resume will have on a hiring manager…

1. **Create first half excellence:** HANDS DOWN, the most important part of your resume is the first half of your resume on the first page. Remember, you typically will only have 6.25 seconds to capture the attention of a potential hiring authority. On the first half of your resume, you want to make sure that your resume is filled with pertinent keywords/skill-sets that are described on the job description. You want to make sure that it is VERY EASY for ANYONE to understand that you are CLEARLY a match for the role that you're applying for, regardless if it is the hiring manager, recruiter or HR professional looking at your resume.

2. **Bullet points are your best friend:** You want to avoid having a lot of paragraphs in your resume. Even if your resume is absolutely phenomenal and a hiring professional decides that they want to read much more of your resume, they're not going to want to read your resume like they would have to a book. You want to make sure that you use bullets and effectively articulate your experience in a way that is relevant for the job that you're currently applying for.

3. **Make your resume keyword rich:** As a Headhunter, I can promise you that keywords really matter. Another ugly truth about the employment process is that hiring professionals aren't going to search very hard to try and understand the potential value that you can bring to their company. Because of how busy everyone is nowadays, if you don't make it super easy for people to see that you fit the mold of what they're looking for on every single page of your

resume, then they will likely end up passing on you and going to the next candidate. It is your responsibility to make sure that every page of your resume is keyword rich and in strong alignment with the skills and competencies that the Hiring Manager is looking for from an ideal candidate.

4. **Focus on numbers, skills and/or accomplishments:** A big mistake that I see a lot of candidates make when writing their resumes is that they fill their resume with a lot of fluff that doesn't really add value to their resume. They'll say things like, "I'm a team player that believes in having a great attitude that creates a positive work environment". While having a great attitude is very important for any job, it doesn't really help you from a resume perspective. When hiring managers are looking at your resume, they're not trying to figure out how great your personality is. They're literally only focused on answering one question-- ARE YOU COMPETENT? When they pick up your resume, they're only trying to see if you actually have the skills that can help them solve their problems. That's it! With that in mind, you want to make sure that you focus on showing numbers, skills, and/or accomplishments that ultimately end up positioning you as a highly skilled candidate that's in great alignment with the needs of this position.

<u>CREATE A CONTROLLED ATTENTION GETTING STRATEGY</u>

T.U.T ACTION STEP #9: 1) Write an irresistible introduction in the form of a phone script, email, letter, etc. 2) Apply for the job 3) Immediately execute your initial attention getting strategy.

Getting attention for yourself is the single most important factor in your job interview process success. If you can't get attention for yourself, then it really doesn't matter how good you are from a resume, skill or attitude perspective. Since getting attention for yourself is very important, you want to make sure that you don't leave this step of the job interview process up to chance.

Most candidates for any job do the bare minimum when it comes to getting the attention of the HDM. Most candidates will apply through the company website for a position, and then cross their fingers and hope that someone notices their resume. While there is the possibility that this approach can work... I definitely don't take this type of approach when applying for a job, and I wouldn't recommend that you take this approach either. Here are the steps that I would recommend you taking to get the attention of a Hiring Manager...

1. **Write an irresistible introduction in the form of a phone script, email, letter, etc:** An irresistible introduction is simply a way of communicating your interest in a job in such a way that a hiring professional will be immediately interested in considering you as a potential candidate for consideration. Go to www.RodneyHughes.com/irresistibleintro to get a sample message that you can use for this introduction.

2. **Apply for the job:** This is a very important part of the employment process. Even though you're going to proactively reach out to the hiring manager with a message that is designed to get his or her attention, you still want to make sure that you go through the typical employment process and apply for the job. Some companies

have to follow a strict procedure when it comes to hiring people, so you don't want to bypass this part of the employment process.

3. **Immediately execute your attention getting strategy:** Once you've prepared your irresistible introduction to get the attention of the hiring authority that you're planning on connecting with, you want to apply for the job and then immediately execute on your attention-getting strategy using your irresistible introduction. This is where your initial planning will be very useful for you. Now you want to get the hiring professionals attention so you can become an actual blip on the radar of this person. Here are some of the ways that you can go about communicating with a hiring professional initially:

- **Making a cold call to the Hiring Manager/HR representative**
- **Emailing the Hiring Mgr/HR rep**
- **Sending a letter to the Hiring Mgr/HR rep**
- **Sending a social media message to a Hiring Mgr/HR rep**
- **Sending a Linked In message to the Hiring Mgr/HR rep**

"EVERYONE IS IN SALES. TO ME, JOB TITLES DON'T MATTER; EVERY EMPLOYEE MUST THINK ABOUT SALES. IT'S THE ONLY WAY ANY COMPANY CAN STAY IN BUSINESS."

~ Harvey Mackay

CHAPTER 14:

The Secrets To INTERVIEWING MASTERY

•••••

Once you've successfully gotten a hiring authority's attention... You must then begin the process of helping this hiring authority understand the real value that you bring to the table. Building value in the job interview process is all about effectively selling yourself. You have to sell the hiring authority and any other key stakeholders that you're the solution that they've been looking for.

MASTERING THE TELEPHONE INTERVIEW

T.U.T ACTION STEP #10: 1) Understand the purpose of a telephone interview 2) Prepare for excellence 3) Be an authentic problem solver 4) Execute the triple C's. 5) Avoid the 3 major pitfalls of a telephone interview.

Once you've successfully became a blip on the radar of a hiring manager, the next logical step in the job interview process is the telephone interview. The telephone interview is very significant because this is where you get to demonstrate your competency for the role you applied for. I'm about to share with you the 4 key things you will want to keep in mind when going through your telephone interview.

1. Understand the purpose of a telephone interview: As a candidate, you must understand that there is only one purpose of a telephone interview--to move the process forward to a face-to-face interview. Period! A huge mistake that I've seen some candidates make is trying to accomplish too much in the telephone interview process.

You must understand that the typical telephone interview is going to last approximately 15 minutes – 1 hour. Because of this limited amount of time, there's only so much information that you'll actually be able to surmise from such a brief conversation. Analyzing an employment opportunity strictly based on a telephone interview is much like analyzing the mass of an iceberg by only looking at what's visible above water. You'll be lucky if you can even get a 10 - 20% understanding of what this job opportunity has to offer you. That's why you only want to focus on selling yourself well enough to get invited in for a face-to-face interview. That's where you'll be able to get a full appreciation for what the opportunity has to offer.

2. Prepare for excellence: Well before your telephone interview, you're going to want to scope out a location where you can have privacy, quietness, and a very strong telephone signal. You never want to try and find a great place to conduct your telephone interview moments prior to the call because you run the chance of running into technical difficulties. You also want to make sure that you get to your ideal location at least 10 minutes prior to the call. You want to be in a calm state prior to the call so you don't end up being flustered when you start your call off.

3. Be an authentic problem solver: Again, the only reason any hiring authority would ever hire someone is because they want to solve a problem.

Before any hiring authority would ever trust that you can help them solve their problems, they must first trust you. I always recommend that you focus on being authentic when you're speaking to people in the employment process. Oftentimes, candidates will try to be something that they're not in the employment process, and they don't realize that most people can see straight through their acting.

Be normal when you're interviewing, but just make sure that you're putting your best foot forward. By being authentic, it will make it easier for people to accept your ideas even if they don't completely agree with your position. Not only do you need to be authentic, but you also need to focus on helping them solve their problems from an authentic perspective. If you truly want to help the hiring authority that you're speaking with solve their problems, you'll create a natural chemistry that will help you exponentially increase your odds of having a successful telephone interview.

4. Execute the triple C's: When communicating with a hiring authority in the telephone interview process, you want to make sure that you execute the triple C's: Clear, Concise, and Compelling. Typically, when a hiring authority is conducting a telephone interview, they're consciously or subconsciously trying to determine how well you communicate. Nobody wants to work with someone that's difficult to communicate with.

As mentioned, you do not have a ton of time to make a great impression on a telephone interview. You also don't have a lot of time to go super in-depth with every single answer. Therefore, you must learn the subtle art of brevity-- how to articulate your ideas in a very clear, concise, and compelling way. The idea here is to always answer questions in a very direct way without rambling, but also making sure that you give enough details to avoid coming across in a cryptic manner. This truly is an art. The best piece of advice I can give you is to follow your gut while communicating with the hiring authority. If you feel like you're rambling, you probably are. If that's the case, then you need to wrap it up quickly.

5. Avoiding the 3 major pitfalls of a telephone interview: The three major pitfalls of any telephone interview are current compensation, compensation expectations, and relocation willingness. I consider these areas pitfalls because if you don't answer these three potential questions properly, you run the chance of having your employment consideration come to an abrupt halt. I've seen great candidates answer one of these three questions wrong and saw how hiring managers did not want to proceed with considering that candidate because of it. It seems pretty petty, but I assure you that this is happening every single day. Here are some ways that I would recommend addressing each of these areas...

- **Current compensation:** If a hiring authority were to ask me what my current compensation is in the telephone interview phase of the job interview process, I would just come straight out and provide a high-level summary of what I may have been earning at that time. As an example, if asked about my current compensation, I may respond with something like this: "Thanks for asking. I'm currently earning a base salary of $30,000, and I make an annual target bonus of 10% with other fringe benefits."

The reason I would approach it this way is because I've seen too many times where candidate have been told by "they", whoever the hell "they" are, that they should never share their current compensation for the fear that a company may not pay them on the highest range because of what they're currently earning. The ugly truth is that there is some validity to that argument in some instances. Even with that being the case, I would still answer that question the way it is answered above because I've seen where candidates have tried to avoid it and have it backfire on them tremendously. I've seen hiring authorities respond unfavorably because someone tried to avoid answering that question directly. Typically, when candidates just come straight out and answer that question, I've seen them come out on top way more than if they had been evasive with that question.

****Although I would **personally** answer this question this way if I were interviewing for a job, I would be knocking on the door of negligence if I didn't at least make you aware of some very significant changes in certain state laws (regarding this specific topic) at the time of writing this book. According to Bloomberg, California, Oregon, Massachusetts, New York, Pennsylvania, & Delaware are either effective or are becoming effective as states where employers cannot legally ask you what you're earning. I personally think that this law has great merit. Women have been earning less than men when you look at hardcore statistics, and something definitely needs to be done to even the playing field. I would totally encourage you to do research on this subject as a candidate, as you need to be aware of state law in your state.*

The reason why I would personally answer this question is because I'm aware of how some hiring authorities may perceive my evasiveness, regardless of the law. I'M NOT recommending that you do what I would personally do in this situation because I think it is important that you make your own decisions about legal matters after consulting with a licensed legal professional, but I do want you to understand a potential ugly truth about this particular line of questioning. Although I'm definitely not saying that it's right, some hiring authorities can potentially take evasiveness of this question as a sign that a particular candidate is not trustworthy, and it could potentially work against that candidate in the consideration process. While

I'm just speaking to you from a position of hypothetical scenarios, this is the type of stuff that I think about when preparing for avoiding pitfalls in the employment process.

- **Compensation expectations:** This is literally the only time in the entire job interview process where I would personally be evasive. I personally feel like I would be losing if I throw out any number at this early juncture in the job interview process. If I say a number that's too high, then I haven't had a chance to really build my value and they may decide that I'm out of their compensation range and not worth the additional investment. If I say a number that is too low, then they may question the true value that I can offer, or worse, they just might give me what I asked for and I would have left a potentially significant amount of money on the table. My personal rule of thumb here is that if I throw out a number, I lose!

If asked this question, I would likely respond by saying something like, "Thanks for asking. At this time, I'm not prepared to provide an accurate answer to this question. I'm very interested in this opportunity, and I'm looking to make a long-term decision. There are other factors, other than just compensation, that I'm considering in this long-term decision. I don't have enough information at this time to make an accurate determination of a fair compensation." I would say something along those lines because no one can fault you for wanting to make a long-term decision. The company wants to deal with someone who is interested in making a long-term decision, but this explanation also gives them a logical explanation for why you're not ready to throw out a number.

While this is definitely an approach I would personally take in this situation, it's still not guaranteed that a hiring authority would let you off the hook this easy. Some hiring stakeholders *(especially HR)* may want to dig a little deeper. They may push you for an answer. In that case, I ALWAYS believe in stating a number that is on the high side of normal. For this reason, it is always a good idea to do as much research as possible to determine a general range of what people are earning in similar positions. I would always ask on the high side of normal because you can always negotiate downward if they're not willing to accept your number, but once you've stated you'll be fine with settling for a low number, it's almost impossible for you to go higher and get more money after that. You can always go down, but it's like trying to climb Mt. Everest trying to go up.

- **Relocation willingness:** While this might not seem like a huge telephone interview pitfall, I assure you that I've seen numerous people get dinged because they weren't able to convince a HDM that they would be willing to relocate for the opportunity. If an opportunity requires a candidate to relocate, you need to understand that a HDM is going to want to feel VERY CONFIDENT that a candidate is willing to relocate before they make an investment to bring that candidate in for a face-to-face interview.

If asked about relocation, I would personally answer like this. "Yes. I'm definitely willing to relocate for the right opportunity." I wouldn't hesitate! I would come straight out and try to instill a high degree of confidence in the hiring authority's mind about this subject because it's an unnecessary obstacle that can be avoided. Even if you don't know all of the information you need to know, answering the question this way would allow me to instill confidence without lying. If I'm engaged in an interview process with a company that would require me to relocate, then of course I would be willing to relocate for the "right opportunity". Even though I know this, it is my responsibility to translate that sense of certainty to the hiring manager so he/she can feel comfortable about moving me forward in the interview process; which by the way, is the purpose of the telephone interview for you as a candidate.

SUCCESS STARTS THE NIGHT BEFORE

T.U.T ACTION STEP #11: 1) Prepare to dress for the success you desire 2) Prepare any necessary documentation/collateral that you may need the night before your interview 3) Set multiple alarms and go to sleep early

Now that you've successfully completed your telephone interview and made a favorable impression on the HDM, it's time to get prepared for the face-to-face interview.

1. Prepare to dress for the success you desire: I have a simple rule of thumb when it comes to dressing for a face-to-face interview-- dress like a senator or high-ranking government official. If you're not too sure how these people dress, then do a quick Google search to get an idea. These government officials are great to pattern yourself after *(from a dressing perspective)* because they typically are great examples of what professionally SAFE dressing looks like. You'll almost never see these people underdressed or overdressed because they understand the importance of dressing well. They know that their outfit can significantly impact their ability to influence others.

There have been times in my life when I didn't have the nice dress clothes that I needed to have to dress like a conservative senator, and I chose to either borrow the money or put the purchase of new clothes on my credit card because I knew how important my outfit was in this process. Once I have my clothes picked out, I make sure that I lay them out somewhere in my house in a nice and neat manner so all I'll have to do is put them on when I wake up in the morning. Preparing your clothes in advance can help you cut down on some of the stress/anticipation that you may feel while getting ready for your interview.

2. Prepare any necessary documentation/collateral that you may need the night before your interview: When I'm getting ready for an interview, I make it a point to print off any documentation that would aid me in the actual interview the night before. Because I view the interview process as being very similar to the sales process, I approach it as if I'm interested in closing the deal that day. While that may not actually happen, I don't want to be in a position where a job offer has to be delayed because I didn't bring the necessary documentation to the interview. You have to remember that the HDM doesn't want to continue interviewing people if he/she has found the right candidate (i.e. you). By printing off the right documentation before the interview, you give that HDM even more incentive to take action on the spot.

Here is a list of things that I typically bring to an interview:

- Multiple copies of my resume on very nice paper
- Any certifications/awards that may be helpful
- A list of business/personal references that you have vetted and approved
- Identification: License, Passport, Birth Certificate & Social Security Card

- Any specific instructions the company may have given you prior to your interview

- Anything else that you think might be required or helpful

3. Set multiple alarms and go to sleep early: Regardless of if you have an early interview scheduled or one later in the day, I would recommend that you set multiple alarms in the morning as early as possible, so you can practically guarantee that you get up on time. I would also make sure that one or two of those alarms are either on your phone or on some other device that doesn't require electricity in order to function. I say this because you have to plan for the worst-case scenario. If the power happens to go out, you don't want to be in a position where you end up getting a late start, or worse, getting to your interview late. This is why you must schedule multiple alarms early enough that you guarantee that you don't have this situation.

Once you've scheduled multiple alarms, I would recommend you going to sleep early. Regardless of the timing of your interview, I think it is important for you to get the proper rest before heading into such an important day. Remember: the actions that you take during your interview will ultimately lead to a several thousand-dollar decision being made regarding you. It doesn't matter if you're interviewing for a minimum wage job or a C-Level role. There is a lot of money at stake when you interview, and even more importantly, there's a lot at stake regarding your overall employment happiness. You want to make sure that you're well rested going into your interview day. You want to be calm and alert, so going to sleep early the night before your interview will help you increase the odds of that happening.

THE GAME HAS BEGUN

T.U.T ACTION STEP #12: 1) Get up and get busy 2) Arrive no later than 30 minutes prior to your interview 3) Write down the name of every person you meet 4) Activate your A-Game from the moment you step out of your car door.

1. **Get up and get busy:** Your multiple alarms go off, and now it's time to get up and get after it. You don't want to procrastinate. When you get up, I would recommend you immediately make up your bed. By getting up and making up your bed, you will be starting your day off by successfully accomplishing something. After you make your bed, I would wash up and then immediately eat something very light for breakfast. You know your body, so make sure that you don't end up eating something that doesn't sit well with your body and/or makes you sluggish. Once you've eaten, I want you to immediately get dressed up in the clothes that you've prepared, pick up the important documentation that you prepared the night before, and get out the door.

2. **Arrive no later than 30 minutes prior to your interview:** Please listen to me clearly. There is literally NO ACCEPTABLE EXCUSE for showing up late to an interview. Period! When I was previously tasked with hiring candidates, this was one of my pet peeves. If someone showed up late to an interview, I wouldn't even waste my time interviewing him or her, regardless of the reasoning for him or her being late. Showing up late to an interview shows that you don't value your time or the time of the hiring authorities that have allocated time to consider you for a position. My personal opinion is that I never trust

anyone who doesn't value time. Time is a non-renewable resource. Once time has been wasted, you can never get it back. So, if someone doesn't respect time, how can you ever expect them to respect your business or anything else for that matter?

I recommend showing up to an interview at least 30 minutes before the interview starts. By showing up early like this, you're able to take this time to relax prior to actually going into the interview. You can pray if you'd like and visualize the success that you desire to have. Also, when you arrive early, it allows you to go into your interview early. When I arrive to interviews 30 minutes early, I always make sure that I go in for that interview at least 10-15 minutes early. Punctuality shows the hiring authorities that you're serious about this job opportunity. Although being punctual might not buy you a lot of brownie points with hiring authorities, I can assure you that being late will be very negatively received and will make your task of getting the job 10 times more difficult. The moral of the story is that you need to focus on being there early to avoid any unneeded drama.

3. **Write down the name of every person you meet:** Although some people may never admit it, most are very impressed when a new acquaintance remembers their name. Their name is very important to them, so when someone else that they don't know finds out their name and remembers it, most people feel really good about that. When I go into an interview situation, I try to always make it a point to write down people's names in my notepad along with their role in the organization. I write it down for two primary reasons. 1) I can always glance at their names before I start speaking to them if I have happened to forget it and 2) By writing their names down, I can find them on LinkedIn and send

them a thank you letter or email once I leave from the interview. I'll dive more into this concept in a later chapter.

4. **Activate your A-Game from the moment you step out of your car door:** From the moment that you step out of your car to go inside for the interview, you need to understand that the game has really just begun. Every single person that you meet from that point until you leave the interview can potentially either positively or negatively impact your success. As soon as you get out of your car, you need to make sure that you keep a positive can-do attitude regarding any person you meet. If you meet someone on an elevator, you want to be warm and pleasant. When you walk through the door of the office, introduce yourself pleasantly to the receptionist, the janitor, or anyone else is in the office. You want to make sure that you let everyone you encounter know why you're there. Regardless of who you meet, you just want to make sure that you come across in a positive fashion and have manners with everything you do.

I'll never forget working for a company where we used a collaborative interviewing process. This particular candidate came to our office to interview with the hiring director, and when he came in the office, he seemed to have somewhat of a condescending attitude towards the receptionist. When he came through the door, I happened to be standing at the receptionist desk, and this guy didn't even acknowledge me. Little did he know, our organization took a collaborative approach towards hiring people. Immediately after he left the office, the hiring director came to both the receptionist and myself to ask us what we thought about him for a management position that he was interviewing for. We both offered a resounding NO! He didn't have his A-Game on that day. He didn't realize the importance of having a great attitude, and therefore ended up missing out on a potentially great opportunity. That's the ugly truth! If you don't bring your A-Game to an interview, then you'll probably miss out on opportunities without ever knowing why.

HANDLING DIFFICULT QUESTIONS IS ALL ABOUT SPIN CONTROL

T.U.T ACTION STEP #13: Don't avoid difficult interview questions, just focus on spin control by overcoming your F.E.A.R.S.

One of the most challenging aspects of any interview process is answering interview questions. How a candidate answers questions can literally make or break a candidate's chances of being selected for a job. You have to remember that hiring authorities are being asked to make very important business decisions based on extremely limited information when they're interviewing potential candidates. For this reason, most interviewers can tend to be non-forgiving when a candidate answers a question wrongly. They do not have the time to explore deep into someone's background. They do not have the luxury of dragging an interview process on with the hopes that a candidate will interview stronger on the next interview. If that company has reached a point where they're actually trying to hire someone, it is because they have problems that they feel they need to address immediately. Therefore, regardless of how skilled you are, it is of the utmost importance that you're prepared to answer any type of interview question that you're asked well.

First, you need to understand the different type of questions that you'll likely run into in an interview situation.

1. Traditional Interview Questions

2. Behavioral Interview Questions

Traditional interview questions are typically very direct questions that sound something like this: What was it about this job that was of interest to you? What would you say your strengths and weaknesses are? What is your motivation for making a change? The key to answering traditional interview questions is that you want to focus on the 3 C's. You want to keep everything coming out of your mouth Clear, Concise, and Compelling. Make sure that they clearly understand your answer. You want to remain concise because if you ramble in your answer, you'll likely lose them in your explanation. And finally, you'll want to make sure that they feel compelled by what you're saying. As an example, if I was asked what my motivation for making a change was, I might respond like this: "Thanks for asking. I've been at my current organization for 10 years now, and while I love what I'm doing everyday, I have a burning desire to contribute at a higher level. When I saw your opportunity, I felt like your needs would be in great alignment with my background, and as I started to learn more about your organization and the exciting things you're doing, I became motivated to explore this opportunity." While this might look a little lengthy in this book, I assure you that if I were speaking this, it wouldn't seem nearly as long. It would come across in a very clear, concise, and compelling way.

Behavioral interview questions are questions that are specifically designed to give an interviewer a glimpse at how a candidate might potentially respond in a given scenario from a behavioral standpoint.

Unfortunately, most interviewers do not warn you when they're about to ask you a behavioral interview question. If you don't want to be blindsided with a difficult behavioral interview question, then you must pay close attention to the signs. If an interviewer ever says something like, "Tell me a time when... Give me an example... Imagine a time when... Describe a time when...", then you're likely about to be asked a behavioral interview question. Prepare to answer their question confidently.

This style of questioning can be found at any level of an interview, but it's typically always found in interview processes where candidates would be responsible for making judgments on behalf of the company. Here are a few examples of behavioral interview questions, "Tell me about a time you were under a lot of pressure. What was going on, and how did you get through it? Describe a time when it was especially important to make a good impression on a client. How did you go about doing so? " These types of questions can really trip up or even cause fear in the best candidates, if they're not prepared to answer these types of questions.

I've come up with an acronym that has helped me effectively handle these types of questions, and hopefully it will help you do the same as it has helped other people that I've coached. When it comes to answering behavioral interview questions, you have to overcome your F.E.A.R.S.

F – State the FACTS

E – EXPLAIN what happened

A – Describe what ACTIONS you took

R – What was the RESULT of your actions

S – Always SPIN the conversation back positive

Let me give you an example of how this works...

Question: Tell me about a time when you and your Manager disagreed about a business decision that ended up negatively impacting your results. How did you respond?

Answer: *(Using the overcome your F.E.A.R.S methodology)*

F = Thanks for asking. In my previous job, I specialized in selling workshop seats to our various public workshops. Our company also had other sales professionals that focused on selling private training and consulting services to our bigger clients. After speaking with the private training/consulting sales professionals, my manager thought it would be good for the business if he allowed those sales professionals to sell public workshop seats as well as having me specialize in doing the same thing.

E = Because of this decision, the following year my numbers ended up dropping significantly because those other sale professionals ended up closing business that I was previously responsible for.

A = After having such a bad year, I decided that I was going to call a meeting with my manager and show him a statistical breakdown of why this approach wasn't best for the overall company.

R = Even after meeting with him and making my case, I wasn't able to convince him to change this policy.

S = Once I realized that I wasn't going to be able to change his mind, I decided to focus on my controllables. I decided to create my own prospecting plan that was going to allow me to reach more qualified prospects in less time. Once I created that prospecting plan and started focusing on aggressively executing that plan, I was able to start exceeding my quota again-- even though I was working in a system that was not designed for me to have maximum success. It was really a blessing in disguise because I learned that I always have the power to get great results even when I don't feel like the odds are stacked in my favor.

Do you see how effective using the "overcome your F.E.A.R.S" approach can work for you when answering difficult behavioral interview question? I came up with this acronym because I personally used to hate answering these types of questions. I used to always feel like the interviewer was trying to lead me into a trap. I felt like they were purposely trying to make me position myself in a light that wasn't going to help me in the interview process. After I learned how to overcome my F.E.A.R.S, everything changed. I started to look forward to answering these difficult questions because I knew that I had a system for answering a question strongly regardless of the question. Here are a few other things you might want to keep in mind that can help you answer any type of difficult interview questions.

- **Prior to going on an interview, it would be a good idea to think about a complex project that you successfully led to completion over the last 6 – 12 months:** It needs to be a project that you led. No one cares to hear about a project that someone else led. You need to have successfully accomplished a goal. As an example, if you were applying for a management job, the interviewers aren't going to want to hear that you solved a problem with an employee by firing them. They're going to want to hear how you used your skills to turn around an underperforming employee. And lastly, don't ever give them an example from 5-10 years ago. I've seen candidates get dinged in an interview because they used an example that was very old and not relevant.

- **Think about the person that's asking you the question:** Remember that the only reason why someone would hire anyone else is because they want to solve a problem. With that in mind, you need to understand that each person you speak to in the job interview process carries a different perspective about the problem(s) that your role is being interviewed to solve. You should always approach answering a question from the perspective of helping that person understand why you would be an ideal fit for the team. You need to understand that a VP and a sales person can ask the same exact question, but they're both looking at that question from their own individual perspective. It's your job to figure out what perspective they're coming from and do your best to cater to that perspective.

- **Don't be afraid to ask for time to gather your thoughts:** NEVER rush to answer a question. If someone asks you a difficult interview question (specifically a difficult behavioral interview questions) don't be afraid to ask him or her for a brief moment to gather your thoughts. It's perfectly normal to feel slightly uncomfortable being totally quiet while you gather your thoughts. Remember: one really bad answer to a question can potentially eliminate you from the consideration process. You'd rather be safe than sorry, so if you feel like you need a little time to gather your thoughts, don't be afraid to ask for more time.

- **Don't be afraid to incorporate humor into your answer:** I have personally found that comedic relief in the interview process can be extremely valuable if used sparingly and effectively. I would warn you though-- If you have a sense of humor that most people don't find that funny, you're probably going to be better off not incorporating humor in the interview process. It's way too risky! But... If you *can* successfully incorporate humor, you can end up winning over some HDMs. Regardless of their title, they're still just human beings that have problems just like us. They like having a good laugh just like everyone else. However, I would recommend you only incorporating humor that you're sure wouldn't offend anyone. If you opt to use more risky humor, then understand that you're really gambling with your future with the company.

Although I wouldn't recommend being risky, I have done so in past interviews and thankfully it ended up working out. I was interviewing with a Fortune 500 company once before, and the HDM mentioned that it looks like I've accomplished quite a bit in my sales career. She then went on to say, "I'm sure you've experienced ups and downs in the selling profession. What have you done when you've experienced a lull in your performance that helped you turn things around and start getting great results again?" I paused for a moment to gather my thoughts, and then I responded by saying, "Thanks for asking me that question. Would you like to know the absolute, fastest way to end up on an antidepressant in the sales profession?" As you can probably imagine, the hiring manager was quite confused at my response, but nonetheless she and her colleagues started laughing almost immediately. I went on to say, "The easiest way to end up on an antidepressant is to pay close attention to all the NO's that you get while you're trying to prospect for potential clients." I went on to teach this hiring manager my philosophy on prospecting, and although she got a good initial laugh, she was very impressed by my approach and response to her question. Do you see how strategically incorporating humor into the interview process can differentiate you from all your competition and allow you to gain a potential competitive advantage?

> "PEOPLE HAVE A NEED FOR CERTAINTY – AND THAT NEED FOR CERTAINTY IS IN EVERY HUMAN BEING. CERTAINTY THAT YOU CAN AVOID PAIN. CERTAINTY THAT YOU CAN AT LEAST BE COMFORTABLE. IT'S A SURVIVAL INSTINCT"

~ Tony Robbins

CHAPTER 15:

Creating a SENSE OF CERTAINTY

•••••

Getting attention and answering questions well will definitely help you increase your odds in the job interview process, but your ultimate goal of interviewing should be to create a sense of certainty in the minds of any HDM that you're the ideal candidate of choice.

CLOSING THE INTERVIEW LIKE A CHAMPION

T.U.T ACTION STEP #14: 1) Only ask position related questions 2) A future-pacing question is like having a cheat code 3) Reassure and articulate your alignment 4) Finish very strong with a smile on your face

Only ask position related questions: Now that you've answered all the questions that the interview person or team has thrown your way, it's time to close out the interview and do your best to create a sense of certainty in the minds of the decision maker(s). Assuming that you did well in the interview, they may ask you if you have any questions for them about the job, company, etc. You never want to say that you don't have any questions, but you also don't want to ask dumb questions. Never ask about vacation, benefits, pay, etc. All of those types of questions can be addressed after they've confirmed that they intend on extending you an offer. Until then, asking questions of this nature don't add value to your ultimate goal of getting the job. I would focus on asking questions that show that you're genuinely interested in helping them solve their problems. Here are a few examples of good questions that can help you come across in a valuable way…

- How does this role ultimately fit into the scope of what your long-term goals are?
- What is the most successful person in this position currently doing differently?
- Is there anything in my background that makes you concerned about my ability to be successful in this role?
- If you had a chance to do things differently from the moment you joined this organization, that you feel would have made you more successful in this role, what would you have done differently?

A future-pacing question is like having a cheat code: Wouldn't it be cool if you could snap your fingers and instantly know exactly what a HDM was looking for in an ideal candidate? Or better, wouldn't it be super cool if you could snap your fingers and instantly know what it would take to be considered as the very best hiring decision that a HDM has ever made prior to leaving an interview? Well, I have great news for you! Although I can't show you how to snap your fingers and figure out this information, I can show you how to ask a question that I call a "future-pacing question" that will accomplish the exact same result.

Here's what a future pacing question sounds like…

"Mr. or Mrs. {Decision Maker's First Name}. Let's imagine that right here, and right now, you decided that I was your ideal candidate that you decided to hire me on the spot. Fast forward to 2 years from today. Now, let's say that I have met and far exceeded your expectations. Better yet, let's imagine that I was literally the best hiring decision that you've ever made up to this point. Can you help me understand what was I able to accomplish specifically that would make you feel this way?"

This question is almost like the closest thing you'll find to pure magic in the job interview process. Let's take a closer analysis of this question and find out what makes it such a great tool.

1. **The Positioning:** You should always save this question for your second to last question that you ask because it will practically guarantee you that you'll end your interview on a very strong and positive note.

2. **The Structure:** The structure of this question is very important. I don't just come straight out and ask the HDM what he or she would need to see from a candidate to consider him or her as their best hiring decision ever. If I asked it that way, I would probably get an answer, but it would likely not be a very strong or compelling answer. What really makes this question so powerful is the structure of the question. You want to always start by setting the stage so the HDM can easily visualize what their best candidate ever looks like,

and then you end with an open-ended question that will inspire him or her to go into great details explaining exactly what he or she would expect from someone who was able to accomplish such great things.

3. **The Psychology:** What makes this question somewhat magical is really the psychology behind the question. By simply asking the future-pacing question, you're forcing the HDM to not only visualize what it would take for a candidate to be considered as their best hiring decision ever, but simultaneously, you're forcing that person to view YOU as that best hiring decision ever before they even decide to officially extend an offer to you. Wouldn't you want a hiring decision-maker to view you as the best hiring decision they've ever made? Well now you can, and all you have to do is ask a future-pacing question.

Reassure and articulate your alignment: Once you've asked the future-pacing question, now it is time to activate your active listening and dictation skills. You want to make sure that you capture the exact bullet points that are described by that HDM. Once you've captured that information, then you want to let that HDM know that you were paying close attention to what they said. You want to repeat back to them exactly what they said and then confirm with him or her that you accurately captured their answers to that question. Once the HDM acknowledges that you have correctly captured that information, then you want to immediately follow up by addressing each one of those answers and reassure the HDM that your background is in alignment with the things that he or she has mentioned. You also want to make sure that you reassure the HDM that if you don't currently have the skills needed to exceed his or her expectations that you will immediately get to work so you can accomplish that goal.

I can't begin to emphasize how important this piece of the process is. This is PURE SELLING. Have you ever heard that expression that people don't want to be sold; they want to buy? That statement is absolute NON-SENSE! People want to be SOLD! They want to be convinced that they are making the right decision. Again, these hiring professionals are being tasked with making extremely important decisions in their business based on very little information. It is your responsibility to sell them on why you're the man or woman for the job! They've already given you all of the firepower you need to be able to sell them effectively since you've asked them the future-pacing question. Now, all you have to do is mirror back to them why you feel that you can live up to that high standard. If you can do that in a compelling way, then the HDM will likely trust that you're the person that can get the job done!

Finish very strong with a smile on your face: Now that you've asked all of your questions about the position, asked the future-pacing question, and reassured the HDM that you have what it takes to live up to the high standard that they articulated, you have to finish strong with a smile on your face. Before you leave the interview, I want you to look the decision maker straight in their eyes and say something along these lines, "I really appreciate your time today, and I want you to know that I'm very excited about this job opportunity. I feel I can help you accomplish great things in this role, and I want you to know that I want this job! What would the next steps be to be selected for this role?" This is what I call going for the close. This should always be your very last question.

You want to know something pretty amazing? I've interviewed many people over my career. As a Headhunter, I've worked with all types of HDMs. Through all of this interview process experience, I can literally only think of one person I haven't trained that actually asked for the job before leaving the interview. This is pretty baffling now that I think about it! It's crazy to think about how much work some candidates have invested into a job interview process, and then they leave an interview without proving their interest in the position by asking for the role.

This chapter is all about creating certainty in this part of the job interview process. I've seen way too many situations where candidates leave from an interview and the company has no idea if the candidate really wants the job. I've even seen situations where a company has liked a strong candidate, but they elected not to extend an offer because they weren't sure if that candidate would actually accept their offer if they extended one. You need to understand that companies are truly striving for a sense of certainty in the job interview process. Never leave from an interview that you genuinely would be interested in taking without making sure that the company knows that you're interested in the role. They may still offer you the position, but it would absolutely suck if you did almost everything right and then ended up missing out on the role simply because they weren't certain that you would accept the job.

"DILIGENT FOLLOW-UP AND FOLLOW-THROUGH WILL SET YOU APART FROM THE CROWD AND COMMUNICATE EXCELLENCE"

~ John C. Maxwell

CHAPTER 16:

The MAGIC Is In The FOLLOW UP

•••••

In my experience, most candidates never end up following up after a face-to-face interview. They walk away from an interview with their fingers crossed hoping that the company will call them and offer them a job. Little do they realize, the best place to gain a competitive advantage over the other candidates is when you follow up after an interview.

HOW TO FOLLOW UP AND MAKE YOURSELF UNFORGETTABLE

T.U.T ACTION STEP #15: 1) Never leave an interview without knowing the next steps and getting people's business cards if possible. 2) Since hi-tech is so popular, I want you to focus on high-touch with the decision maker 3) Email every key stakeholder and connect with them on LinkedIn 4) Find creative ways to stay in touch until a decision has been made.

Never leave an interview without knowing the next steps and getting people's business cards if possible: In the event that you close out your interview strong by asking for the job and they tell you that they're still considering other candidates or have other things that they need to do before making their final decision, you want to be prepared to go into follow up mode. You should always make it a point to ask what the next steps will be in the job interviewing process. Asking this question will oftentimes give you some strong insight as to how well you did in the interview. At the very least, by asking this question, you'll be able to reduce your anxiety about how long their consideration process might be. Once you've gotten an idea of what the next steps are from a consideration perspective, make sure that you don't leave out of their office without at least getting a few people's business cards. Business cards are very important because it will give you pertinent information that will help you follow up successfully.

Since hi-tech is so popular, I want you to focus on high-touch when you're following up with the ultimate decision maker: I would ALWAYS recommend that you follow up any face-to-face interview you go on with sending a note to the hiring manager, thanking him or her for their time and emphasizing your interest in the role. It amazes me how many people go on an interview and do not even have the decency to send a thank you email after interviewing. Please understand that manners really do go a long way in life, but especially in the job interview process.

In a day and time when hi-tech is so popular, I would recommend you leveraging high-touch as it relates to making your initial follow up with the hiring manger after your interview to thank him or her. Nowadays, there's a lot of noise in the email inboxes of most decision makers within companies. While there's a lot of noise in the digital communication mediums, there's hardly any noise in their mailboxes. For this reason, I would recommend sending the hiring manager a letter thanking him or her for taking time to interview you and reassuring that hiring manager that you're prepared to come in and make a great impact.

When I'm preparing to go into a face-to-face interview, I always make it a point to write a thank you letter template before I go in because I know that I plan to mail that letter afterwards. Once I get out of the interview, I will immediately tweak that thank you letter to make sense for the conversations that I had with the hiring manager. Then I will print that letter off, sign it, and then head off to the post office. When I get to the post office, I will ask the postal employee what shipping option I should select to guarantee that my letter would arrive the following morning at the office of the hiring manager. I've received different prices, but I'm always willing to spend whatever I need to spend to send the letter with this level of priority. I'm always willing to do this because I'm making an investment in my future!

This approach has been a secret weapon for me over my career. As mentioned previously, most people never even send a thank you email, much less a signed thank you letter that was sent in priority level mail. Let me ask you something. How many other candidates' do you think are willing to go to these measures to show their appreciation for the opportunity? I assure you that the overwhelming majority of people are only interested in giving the least possible amount of effort to get the highest amount of success. Because I've been willing to go out of my way to WOW the hiring managers that I've wanted to work with, I've always been able to create an extreme competitive advantage for myself by doing things like this.

Email every key stakeholder a thank you email and connect with them on LinkedIn: Now that you've thanked the hiring manager, you're going to want to follow up with and thank the other key stakeholders that you interacted with at the company. As mentioned... Most people go to interviews and never express their appreciation for everyone's time. This is a failure that you can capitalize on. I would figure out the email cadence of each person that I met and then send each individual a personalized thank you email the same day as the interview. After sending out your emails, then I would also go on LinkedIn and connect with anyone that you met that day. You'll be surprised at just how impactful these simple gestures are to the people that you met at the interview, even if they never respond to your email or LinkedIn connection request.

Find creative ways to stay in touch until the decision has been made: Once you've thanked everyone, then you need to go on your calendar and schedule the date at which they said they would make their decision. If the date is relatively soon (ideally 2 weeks or less), then you can schedule a date after that time frame to follow back up with either the hiring manager or the human resources representative that you're communicating with in this process. If they tell you that they're not looking to make a decision for at least a month or two, then you want to find a creative way to stay in touch with the hiring manager so you can stay on the top level of that hiring manager's mind. **Here are a few examples of things you can do to stay top of mind:**

- Email the hiring manager an interesting article, and check on the status of his or her decision-making process.
- Mail the hiring manager a magazine that you think might be of interest to that hiring manager and then follow up.
- Think of a question that is applicable to the role you're interviewing for, and then cold call the hiring manager to ask that question and then follow up

Feel free to be as creative as you'd like when you're trying to figure out a way to follow up. I've always found that if you figure out a creative way to lace your follow up attempts with valuable information that is pertinent to the person you're following up with, they'll rarely ever get annoyed by your follow up attempts. People tend to get annoyed when there is no additional value being offer when someone is following up. Lace your follow up with value, and do your best to stay top of mind until they ultimately make a hiring decision. Hopefully that decision will be in your favor.

"THE BETTER YOU ARE AT COMMUNICATING, NEGOTIATING, AND HANDLING YOUR FEAR OF REJECTION, THE EASIER LIFE IS"

~ Robert Kiyosaki

CHAPTER 17:

How To Get What You REALLY WANT

•••••

In a world where so many people never ask for what they really want, if you do a great job of maneuvering through the job interview process, you deserve the right to at least ask for what you really want.

HOW TO GET THE VERY BEST OFFER

T.U.T ACTION STEP #16: 1) Analyze the fairness of the offer. 2) The best counter response I've ever heard.

Analyze the fairness of the offer: Congratulations! The company you've interviewed with feels like you're the ideal candidate, and they want to make you an offer to join their organization. You've made all the right steps if you've gotten to this point in the process. Although you've gotten to this point, you still have some work to do to ultimately land the job. Once they've extended an official offer to you, you need to be prepared to analyze the fairness of the offer.

You have to realize that it is in the best interest of the company to get the best possible talent at the lowest possible cost. Although this is the goal of every company, it does not mean that every company is going to try to low-ball you. As a matter of fact, I would even say that most companies try their best to extend what they believe is a fair and equitable offer when they're trying to attract top talent. Some companies are even willing to go over and beyond what anyone would consider to be fair.

Although there are many companies that extend fair offers, you must not allow yourself to be naive or foolish during this part of the job hiring process. There are some companies out here that will gladly low-ball a candidate with the express intention of saving money. I've actually worked with companies that use an initial low-ball offer as a strategic way of intentionally trying to give a candidate the lowest possible offer. In my opinion, this is the dumbest thing a company could do, but as a candidate, you need to understand that there are hiring authorities/companies that think very similar to predators in the wild when it comes to getting great talent.

When you receive an offer, I want you to analyze the offer in its entirety. I don't want you to go into reading your offer thinking that the company is going to automatically try to take advantage of you, but I do want you to analyze the entire offer and draw your best conclusion. You have to look at the entire offer because every company tends to approach theirs differently. Some companies believe in paying very well up front with guaranteed income, and then not offering much on the back-end. Some companies believe in paying lower up front, but then having an amazing back-end earning potential based on performance. Some companies believe in trying to create a very balanced offer that is very fair, and some companies simply believe in low-balling.

The point here is that every company approaches the offer process differently, so you're going to have to use your reasoning skills to determine if an offer is fair and equitable for you. NEVER... And I do mean NEVER... Allow yourself to settle for an unfair offer because you need a job. Now that you have the skills that have been taught to you in this book, you don't have to settle for less. With that being said, it is vitally important that you don't be unreasonable in your analysis of a job offer. I've seen some candidates turn down amazing offers because they had unreasonable expectations. After fully considering an offer in its entirety, I want you to determine if you feel like the offer is acceptable. If it is, then don't ask for more. If you feel that an offer is unacceptable, then you need to determine what you feel would be a fair and equitable offer based on reality.

I remember one woman I knew that was fresh out of college, and had to get a job so she could start paying back her student loans. She was from Alabama, but wanted to move to Atlanta. To make a long story short, she got interviewed and the company presented her with an offer. The offer was several thousand dollars less than the average. Although she needed the job, she knew that she was worth more than what was being offered. One thing you have to be prepared to do is walk away. Never let anyone sell you short. Because of the low-ball offer, she declined the position. Luckily, the company didn't want to take no for an answer. They asked her what she wanted, and she gave her the absolute minimum that she would accept. A day later, they not only gave her the minimum, but they offered her a relocation bonus as well.

The best counter response I've ever heard: Let's assume for a moment that you have determined that the offer is unacceptable after you've thoroughly reviewed it in its entirety. If you determine that the offer is way off from what you think would even be doable for you, then you just need to thank them for their time and say that you have decided not to accept the offer. As an example, there's no need to drag things on if you think that a company should have offered you a $100K base and they extended an offer to you of $30K. There's practically no way that you'll be able to find a happy medium if the spread is that wide. This is an extreme example, but I think it makes the point.

If you analyze the offer and the offer doesn't seem too far off the mark, then you owe it to yourself to counter to get what you really want. Oftentimes, countering an offer (aka negotiating) is a process that both candidates and employers don't enjoy participating in. I've seen both candidates and employers approach the negotiation process horribly, and if not careful, I've seen both parties leave the negotiations very bitter. The real goal of negotiating should be to create a situation that both parties feel is mutually beneficial. Since you can't control how the employer is going to respond to negotiating, it is your responsibility to put your best foot forward and get a situation that makes sense for you and your family.

There are many different ways that you can go about going into a counter situation, but I was recently reading an article on www.inc.com (https://www.inc.com/betsy-mikel/how-to-negotiate-a-higher-job-offer-in-just-1-simple-sentence.html) that gave a great suggestion for approaching the negotiation process. Karen Catlin (of https://karenkatlin.com/) suggests using one sentence to negotiate a better offer. Here's what Karen said you should respond with: "If you can get me X, I'll accept the offer right away." Although I have personally never been in a situation where I've had to use this exact verbiage, I believe this is an absolutely genius way of approaching what can be a very tense situation.

Why? As a Headhunter, I can tell you that neither the company nor the candidate ever feel comfortable negotiating. I've heard all kinds of things in negotiation scenarios that prove that both parties hate doing it. **There are a few things that make this response so powerful…**

1. **It's simple:** This response doesn't require you to have a golden tongue. Most people hate negotiating because they feel like they have to be this great orator to be successful at it. With this approach, you don't have to feel that way.

2. **It cuts out the back and forth:** Nobody wants to go back and forth when negotiating. This approach allows the company to know that there is an end in mind. Ultimately, the company just wants the person to say yes. As long as the counter number is within range of being doable, they'll be happy to bump up if they know the candidate will say yes.

3. **You get the real deal:** As a candidate, if a company is unable to match the number that you state, by using this approach, you'll at least get the real deal number that is feasible from the company. By getting the real number, you can make an ultimate decision based on knowing the real numbers. You won't wonder if you left money on the table.

"EVERYBODY WANTS TO BE A BODYBUILDER, BUT NOBODY WANTS TO PUSH THIS OLE HEAVY {CENSORED} WEIGHT"

~ Ronnie Coleman

CONCLUSION:

Take The EASY STREET To Massive Success

● ● ● ● ●

This may seem counterintuitive, but I want you to take the EASY STREET to massive success...

Taking the EASY STREET to massive success is actually very simple. Now that you have acquired the skills necessary to dominate in the job interview process, all you have to do to take the EASY STREET is actually apply the hard skills that most people are too lazy or too fearful to apply. Taking the EASY STREET is really about doing the difficult things that most people aren't willing to do so you can have the things that most people can't have.

It's very sad that so many people never end up tapping into their potential, even though they have the information needed to make a great impact and be successful. My personal belief is that this happens because people are constantly trying to find the easiest path to getting to success without having to do all the difficult actions that will get them there. They don't realize that the HARD STREET to success is oftentimes disguised as the EASY STREET, and the EASY STREET is oftentimes disguised as the HARD STREET.

I want you to make a paradigm shift. Start looking for the difficult actions that most people are trying to avoid, and I want you to have the courage to march down that path and take those actions. Although there will be temporary pain, frustrations, and discomforts, I assure you that that is actually the EASY STREET. That is the best path to getting the greatest success in the least possible amount of time.

The ideas, skills, and techniques that I have shared with you in this book can seem to be very difficult on the surface, especially if you're more introverted in nature. I'm an introvert, and every time I've attempted to apply the strategies in this book, I have had to push through being uncomfortable; but it has ALWAYS been worth it. By simply using the information in this book when I didn't necessarily want to, I have always had great success in less time. This is what taking the EASY STREET is all about, and it is my greatest hope that you will commit from this day forward to taking the EASY STREET with me. I wish you the best on your employment endeavors. Thank you for taking the time to read this book, and I wish you much love, peace and success in the future!

"YOU CAN'T ESCAPE FROM A PRISON UNTIL YOU RECOGNIZE YOU ARE IN ONE. PEOPLE WHO HAVE CHOSEN TO LIVE WITH THE LIMITS OF THEIR OLD BELIEFS CONTINUE TO HAVE THE SAME EXPERIENCES. IT TAKES EFFORT AND COMMITMENT TO BREAK OLD PATTERNS"

~ Bob Proctor

FREE INTERVIEW PREP VIRTUAL TRAINING

•••

Discover extremely effective strategies that will help you seamlessly maneuver the job interview process like a pro!

Dear Success-Minded Friend:

Because you purchased this book, I'm going to give you (FREE) lifetime access to a virtual training platform called INTERVIEW PREP UNIVERSITY. This virtual training platform is specifically designed to walk you step-by-step through the job interview process and help you avoid the major pitfalls that cause most candidates to fail miserably in the job interview process…

Here's a quick glance at what you'll learn in Interview Prep University…

- **COURSE 1:** Interview Scheduling Course
    - Learn how to quickly schedule interviews with top companies.
- **COURSE 2:** Telephone Interview Course
    - Learn how to avoid the common telephone interview mistakes.
- **COURSE 3:** Onsite Interview Course
    - Learn how to effectively sell yourself during a job interview.
- **COURSE 4:** Compensation Course
    - Learn how to negotiate top-dollar when getting an offer.

How to use this virtual course effectively?

The best way to get maximum value from this virtual course is to start by completely reading this book. This book will serve as the foundation for what you're going to learn in this virtual course. Once you've read the book, you can use this platform in various ways. You can go through the whole course in one evening, pace yourself and do a section a day, or jump straight to a certain section of this course that you think is most applicable to your concerns. Remember… This virtual course is designed to supplement the ideas, concepts, and strategies that are shared in this book.

How do you gain instant access to Interview Prep University?

Go to ➔ www.InterviewPrepUniversity.com

RODNEY HUGHES

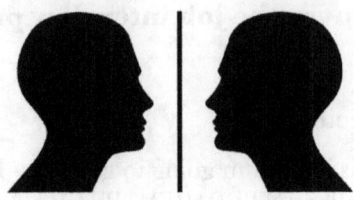

THE
UGLY TRUTH
ABOUT GETTING
HIRED

Author | Professional Speaker | Executive Recruiter

DISCOVER HOW TO LAND THE JOB OF YOUR DREAMS...

REGARDLESS OF THE COMPETITION!

www.ingramcontent.com/pod-product-compliance
Lightning Source LLC
Chambersburg PA
CBHW060528010526
44110CB00052B/2534